BEHIND THE GREEN MONSTER

Red Sox Myths, Legends, and Lore

BILL BALLOU

TRIUMPH
BOOKS

No part of this publication may be reproduced, stored in a retrieval system, or transmitted in any form by any means, electronic, mechanical, photocopying, or otherwise, without the prior written permission of the publisher, Triumph Books, 542 South Dearborn Street, Suite 750, Chicago, Illinois 60605.

Triumph Books and colophon are registered trademarks of Random House, Inc.

Library of Congress Cataloging-in-Publication Data TK

This book is available in quantity at special discounts for your group or organization. For further information, contact:

Triumph Books
542 South Dearborn Street
Suite 750
Chicago, Illinois 60605
(312) 939-3330
Fax (312) 663-3557

Printed in U.S.A.
ISBN: 978–1–60078–191–9
Design by Patricia Frey
Photo credits by AP Images.

CONTENTS

FOREWORD

It's all here: the great seasons, the great games, the great moments, and the great players. And even if some of the above weren't so great, they sure were memorable. Do you remember the time Manny Ramirez cut off Johnny Damon's throw from the outfield even though he stood only 20 feet away? I do. Bill Ballou does. I'll never forget it. It was Manny being Manny, and now that he's gone, Red Sox fans will have to wonder whether there'll be "The Curse of Manny Ramirez" much like "The Curse of The Bambino," which Ballou argues never existed. That's the fun of *Behind the Green Monster*. Bill Ballou is a contrarian—he is a puncturer of myths, the naysayer of conventional wisdom.

What's the most important date in Red Sox history? Most Red Sox fans would argue it was the sale of Babe Ruth to New York. No, no, and no. That's much too negative. Without reading the answer, my response was automatic—the firing of Joe Cronin, whose racist and idiotic tenure as general manager consigned the Sox to almost 20 years of failure. I was floored when Ballou took the argument one step further. In this book, he contends the greatest moment in Red Sox history was the hiring of Dick O'Connell, the man who took over the team and rebuilt it after Cronin was fired. I was amazed. Ballou must be a genius.

Always he brings you back. Remember when Dave Roberts stole second base in the bottom of the ninth of Game 4 against the Yankees in the 2004 playoffs? Everyone remembers it, because when he scored and they beat the Yankees, the Sox were on their way to immortality. But who drove in Roberts with the winning run? Why wasn't his hit as important or memorable as Roberts' stolen base? It's hard to argue with that. The answer: Bill Mueller, who Ballou calls "one of the anonymous Red Sox great players."

Ballou recounts the saga of Matt Young. He came over from Seattle with a spotty record and proceeded to throw a no-hitter for the Sox—in a game he lost 2–1. No one remembers, but the catcher that day was John Flaherty, who started his first game in the major leagues. Flaherty thus became the only catcher to make his debut and catch a no-hitter. Young, by the way, is one of the few pitchers ever to strike out four batters in an inning. Even crazier, the baseball commissioner's office refused to recognize Young's achievement as a no-hitter because he pitched eight, not nine, innings. Fortunately, the Hall of Fame isn't quite so picky.

Everyone knows baseball was not founded by Abner Doubleday and that Babe Ruth didn't call his shot. Along those same lines, if anyone tells you Johnny Pesky held the ball to lose a game in the 1946 World Series, tell them they're crazy. By the way, the right-field foul pole isn't called the "Pesky pole" because of any home runs that Johnny bounced against it. In his entire 10-year career, he only hit 17 homers. It's called the Pesky pole, says Ballou, because it sounds good, and it's a way to honor the lifetime Red Sox star.

There is one trivia question no one can argue: Who was the worst-fielding Red Sox player of all time? The answer: Dick Stuart. Who was the best player ever acquired by the Sox in a trade? He says it's Ray Culp. Personally, I think it was Jason Varitek and Derek Lowe, who were acquired in a trade for Heathcliff Slocum, a journeyman pitcher who sounded like he was invented by Jane Austen.

There is so much to relive in this book. There are the obvious moments: Fisk's home run, Yaz's miraculous September in 1967, the four-in-a-row sweep of the Yankees in 2004. But how about the day in 1951 when Clyde Vollmer hit three home runs in one game? How about Bernie Carbo's pinch-hit home run in the 1975 World Series? Then there was probably the longest home run in the history of the game of baseball. It is marked in the right-field bleachers of Fenway Park with a red seat. Ted Williams hit it. The ball went approximately 514 feet.

Today's players look at the spot and refuse to believe anyone could hit a ball that far. But they did not see Ted play. The greatest player ever to wear a Red Sox uniform, Ted was Superman minus the cape. He was the last man to hit .400. His lifetime batting average was .344 and he hit 521 home runs even though he missed five full seasons fighting in two wars. He would say, "I'm Teddy Effing Ballgame, and I am the greatest hitter who ever lived."

Ted wasn't modest, but he wasn't wrong. Ted's in this book, along with a lifetime of Red Sox memories.

—Peter Golenbock

INTRODUCTION

History is like weather. It is always there, except that some of it is interesting and some of it is not. The Boston Red Sox have had the most interesting weather of any major league baseball team.

The Red Sox won the first World Series. The Red Sox bought, then sold, the greatest baseball player in history, Babe Ruth. They destroyed one dynasty by doing that and created another. They were baseball's best team in the 1910s, its worst in the 1920s.

The Red Sox gave the world Ted Williams, the last .400 hitter and the only Hall of Famer to hit a home run in his last at-bat. The Red Sox played—and lost—the first pennant playoff in American League history. They played—and lost—the first playoff for a division title in American League history.

They went into the final two games of the 1949 season needing to win just one to capture the pennant and lost both. They went into the final two games of the 1967 season needing to win both games to win the pennant and won both.

The Red Sox played and won the greatest World Series game in history—Game 6 in 1975—but lost the World Series. Dave Henderson's home run in Game 5 of the 1986 ALCS sparked one of the most memorable comebacks ever; Boston's loss in Game 6 of that year's World Series is the most devastating World Series loss ever.

The Red Sox lost four straight World Series Game 7s. The Red Sox are the only team to fall behind in a playoff series three games to none and win the series—and against the Yankees, no less. The Red Sox are the team of Ruth and Williams, Carl Yastrzemski and Roger Clemens, and Mike Higgins and Pumpsie Green.

The Yankees may have dominated the American League standings through the year, but the Red Sox have dominated the headlines.

CHAPTER 1

THERE WAS NEVER ANY CURSE

Noah Webster was born in West Hartford, Connecticut, and lived in New Haven, so he spent his life right on the fault line that generally separates Red Sox fans from Yankees fans. Webster was neither, of course, since he died 58 years before the American League was founded.

His legacy was the definition of a word that haunted the Sox for years, though—curse—which he defined as "a source or cause of evil; a scourge."

The Curse of the Bambino is a relatively recent addition to Red Sox lore. It was first used after Boston's stunning defeat in the 1986 World Series, and was then popularized by Dan Shaughnessy's splendid book of that title relating all the misfortune that characterized Sox history in the years after Babe Ruth was sold to the Yankees. Ruth never put a curse on the Red Sox, nor did anyone else, but his sale to New York certainly seems like it was the source or cause of a lot of, let's say, misfortune.

However, the concept of the Curse of the Bambino was always for tourists and amateurs, a catchphrase that condensed four score and six years of history into five words. It became shorthand and nothing more. It was used the same way that people talked about root canals—about as much fun as a root canal—even though most people have never had a root canal and even though with novocaine and sedation dentistry and modern technology root canals don't hurt any more than having a filling.

Curse of the Bambino? It needed no explanation. Everybody knew what you meant and shook their heads knowingly. Really, though, the

Babe Ruth, ca. 1916. Ruth was in the Red Sox starting rotation from 1914 to 1918, pitching in the World Series in 1916 and 1918, before joining the New York Yankees, where he became the Sultan of Swat. (AP Photo)

concept of the Curse of the Bambino was group whining. Throughout its existence, the Boston franchise has been one of the most successful in all of sports both on and off the field. As bad as the bad has been for Red Sox fans, and there has been plenty of bad, the good has been good.

So, what really happened between 1918 and 2004 both good and bad?

In their landmark book, *Red Sox Century*, authors and baseball historians Glenn Stout and Dick Johnson convincingly and logically debunked the whole Curse of the Bambino mythology although doubters

2

remain. There is no question that in the years after the Sox's World Series victory in 1918, owner Harry Frazee conducted a tremendous transfer of baseball wealth from Boston to New York, something akin to the transfer of wealth from the wallets of American drivers to OPEC. And it made the Yankees rich.

However, it was not unprecedented. Philadelphia Athletics owner Connie Mack did something similar twice, once after his 1914 team was swept in the World Series by the Miracle Braves, and then after the stock market crash of 1929 and subsequent Great Depression wiped him out financially. The Red Sox got future Hall of Fame pitcher Herb Pennock and their manager in 1917, Jack Barry, that way. After Tom Yawkey bought the franchise, Boston got Lefty Grove and Jimmie Foxx—one of the greatest pitchers and one of the greatest sluggers ever—in lopsided deals similar to the ones Frazee made with Yankees owner Jacob Ruppert.

To get Grove, Rube Walberg, and Max Bishop in 1933, Yawkey sent $125,000, Rabbit Warstler, and Bob Kline to the A's. To get Foxx and Johnny Marcum in '35, Boston sent Gordon Rhodes, George Savino, and $150,000 to Philly. In the 1950s, after Mack sold the Athletics to Arnold Johnson who moved the franchise to Kansas City, Johnson shipped star after star to the Yankees in deals that never returned him dollar for dollar in baseball value.

Before the free-agent draft began in 1965, that's the way things worked in baseball. That doesn't make Frazee any less guilty of dismantling his team—it just makes him less uniquely sinister.

As it was, the sale of Ruth to the Yankees was the last piece of New York's dynasty puzzle, not the first. Even with Ruth's 29 home runs and 114 RBIs to lead them offensively, the Red Sox finished 13 games behind New York in the American League standings in 1919.

Frazee had begun tearing apart the 1918 champions right after the season ended, and it was actually a good idea. The 1918 World Series title was a gift of sorts, connected chronologically with the dynasty of 1912, 1915, and 1916, but disconnected in most other ways.

The 1918 season was more similar to 1981 and 1994 than the ones that went before it. Participation in World War I took most of the nation's time, energy, and attention, and baseball was an afterthought. The season was almost canceled midway through—Frazee was instrumental in saving it—but the casualty rate for major league rosters was almost as dramatic as the one on the front lines in France.

Aside from Ruth, the starting nines of the 1916 and 1918 Sox had two players in common, shortstop Everett Scott and right fielder Harry Hooper, and two starting pitchers in common, Carl Mays and Dutch Leonard. Otherwise, the 1918 team was built on the run. In that season, the Red Sox were simply better improvisers, and to some extent simply luckier, than anyone else in the American League.

By 1919, the Bill Carrigan Boston dynasty had gotten old and Frazee and his manager, Ed Barrow, recognized it. The first Carrigan standouts they moved were pitcher Ernie Shore and outfielder Duffy Lewis, who had missed all of 1918 in the military. Before that, though, Shore had gone from 19 to 16 to 13 wins in a span of three seasons and Lewis was heading into his thirties. They were both traded to the Yankees and both were, as the Sox projected, near the end of the line.

Frazee's problem wasn't so much that he dumped talent as that he got little or nothing in return. He also lacked a farm system, but nobody had a farm system in those days.

When a franchise began to spiral downwards, it was usually hard to reverse the process. It became a self-fulfilling prophecy—lousy teams meant lousy attendance. Lousy attendance meant less revenue. Less revenue meant less ability to buy good players from the minor league owners who held their contracts. That left people like Frazee one option—they became the minor leagues for the competition, selling off whatever good talent they had accidentally accrued.

Frazee and the Red Sox were not unique in this. Boston's baseball fans knew how it worked only too well.

The once-beloved Braves, who dominated the National League in the 1890s, were decimated by the formation of the American League in 1901. Poor and playing in a tiny, outdated ballpark, the Braves went through a series of owners in the early 1900s and were never contenders. From 1903 to 1912, when James Gaffney bought them and renamed them the Braves, Boston's National League team never finished higher than sixth place.

There were the Miracle Braves of 1914, and that miracle was partly a function of the appearance of the rebel Federal League, but after that it was back to the second division. From 1917 through 1946, the Braves never finished higher than fourth place. Things were the same if you were a St. Louis Browns fan. They finished second in 1902, second in 1922, and won their only pennant in 1944 with major league rosters depleted by World War II.

It was no different if you were a Phillies fan. They won a National League pennant in 1915, then didn't win another until 1950, then didn't win another until 1980, then didn't win another until 2008. That was the way it was in baseball, and in baseball more than any other sport. There were haves and have-nots and it took a lot to change the way things were.

That change usually came in the form of innovation, like the Cardinals creating the farm system under Branch Rickey, or Rickey's Dodgers breaking the color line, or it came in the form of new ownership and new money.

The Red Sox tried the new ownership route when Frazee finally sold the team in the summer of 1923 to a group headed by Bob Quinn, who had helped Phil Ball run the Browns, a team that finally seemed to be turning the corner of respectability. Quinn had the baseball knowledge, but no money. The money came from Palmer Winslow, who made lots of money making lots of glass bottles.

The deal did what a manager does when he takes, say, a great third baseman and turns him into a mediocre first baseman, thus weakening the team at two positions. Having Quinn go from St. Louis to Boston weakened the American League at two franchises. Still, it might have worked for the Red Sox if Winslow had not promptly died, leaving

Quinn with only a few good players, but no farm system in place and no money to buy talent.

It wasn't until Quinn was finally forced to sell to Tom Yawkey that the Red Sox finally left the have-nots for the haves. Yawkey spent plenty of money, and even created a farm system, but he had one gigantic strike against him in trying to create a champion—the Yankees.

No team has ever dominated a major sport the way the Yankees have dominated the American League. Nothing in the National Football League comes close. The Boston Celtics of the NBA had a run that was as good as the Yankees, but fell off worse than the Yankees ever did. The NHL's Montreal Canadiens had the Yankees' same level of dominance for many years, but even they couldn't maintain it for as long as the Bronx Bombers.

Comparing any American League team to the Yankees is like saying Canada has the second-largest army in North America. They are really separate animals. The Red Sox were not the only franchise to suffer in the shadow of the Yankees. From 1921 when the Yanks won their first American League pennant—it's hard to believe, but for the first two decades of their existence, the Yankees weren't much better than the Texas Rangers—to 2004 when the Sox finally won another World Series, not many AL teams whose nicknames didn't rhyme with "Schmankees" won world championships.

The Browns, who became the Orioles, won three. The Athletics, in their various locations, won six. The White Sox won none. The Indians won one. The Tigers won four. The original Senators, who became the Twins, won three.

Part of what became known as the Curse of the Bambino was something much more fundamental to the game of baseball, and that was the law of averages. A .300 hitter doesn't get three hits with every 10 at-bats. He gets six hits in 10 at-bats, then doesn't get any hits in the next 10. It is human nature to figure that if it didn't happen in my lifetime it never happened, and if it happens after I'm gone, who cares? The reality is that since the American League became a major league in

1901, the Red Sox have been one of baseball's most successful teams. It is just that their success was mostly achieved during the early part of their existence and again in the most recent part. In the end, their bottom line looks really good.

If you were a Red Sox fan in the first part of the twentieth century, watching your team win pennants and World Series was a regular event. The Sox won five of the first 15 World Series ever played, and six of the first 18 American League pennants. In the decade starting with 1910, Boston was to Major League Baseball what New York would become in the 1950s. The Red Sox won the World Series in 1912, 1915, 1916, and 1918; the Braves won it in 1914.

That's five world championships in seven years.

Looking at the history of Major League Baseball from 1903, when the first World Series was played—and won by the Red Sox— the Sox's record is very good. Of the original eight American League franchises, the Yankees are by themselves with 39 pennants and 26 World Series titles. After that it is the Athletics with 14 pennants and nine world championships; the Red Sox with 12 pennants and seven world championships; the Tigers with 10 pennants and four World Series titles; the original Senators and Twins with six pennants and three World Series titles; the White Sox with six pennants and three world championships; and the Indians with five pennants and just two World Series titles. Red Sox fans, instead of bemoaning the 86 years between titles, should probably count their blessings.

What certainly contributed to the concept of some sort of supernatural powers at work during the Red Sox's 86 years of frustration was the manner in which they found ways to fail and there was, indeed, some outright bad luck in there.

The bad luck, in chronological order.

1. It began with the sale of Ruth, which was officially done on January 3, 1920. Although Barrow knew at the time that it was a mistake, in large part, the sale of Ruth was looked at by fans and reporters

as something similar to Boston's trade of Manny Ramirez at the deadline in 2008. Ruth had become increasingly difficult to deal with—it was The Babe being The Babe—and even though he led the league in home runs with 29 in 1919, the Red Sox still finished below .500 and Frazee figured the team could finish below .500 without him, too.

What Frazee did not know was that Ruth's ability to hit home runs was not an aberration, it was a revolution. Where Ruth had hit 29 home runs in 1919 playing half of his games in a park where the right-field power alley was more than 400 feet away, the slugger was being shipped to a team that played its home games in the Polo Grounds where it was 256 feet down the right-field line, and to a team that would build its own stadium and tailor right field so that it was just 296 feet from home plate to the seats.

While the sale of Ruth started the drought, a lot happened in the aftermath. In particular was the death of Winslow after Quinn had used the promise of his money to buy the team from Frazee. Winslow became sick in 1924 and withdrew his financial support. He finally died in 1926, and with Winslow's cash gone, Quinn had no resources.

2. When Tom Yawkey bought the team in 1933, it was a great piece of luck for Sox fans, even if the subsequent years contained disappointment. At least the team was out of the basement and competitive again. It took Yawkey's Red Sox 13 years to go from the basement to the World Series, with the Yankees standing in the way for most of that time.

3. When Boston finally did win a pennant and go to a World Series, it was 1946, and that is really where the franchise's string of misfortune began. That World Series against the Cardinals marked the first of four in a row that the Red Sox lost in seven games.

And it was one they should have won, or at least had a chance to win. The Sox took a 3–2 series lead into Game 6 in St. Louis, lost that one, and went to Game 7, also at Sportsman's Park. Boston was on its way to going down quietly and somewhat painlessly. It trailed 3–1 going into the top of the eighth and had the bottom of the batting order coming up. Manager Joe Cronin pinch-hit Rip Russell and Catfish Metkovich, in that order, for catcher Hal Wagner and pitcher Joe Dobson.

Perfect strategy, as Russell singled and Metkovich doubled to put two men in scoring position with nobody out. Wally Moses struck out, then Johnny Pesky lined out, and the runners stayed put, but Dominic DiMaggio doubled both of them in to tie the score in dramatic fashion.

That brought up Ted Williams, but in the final postseason plate appearance of his major-league career, he stranded DiMaggio in scoring position by popping out to second base. Still, Boston had shown a lot of guts, and Cronin some inventive managing, in coming back to forge the tie in the Cardinals' home park. Unfortunately for the Sox as a whole—and DiMaggio, Williams, and Bobby Doerr, none of whom would ever get to the World Series again—it all fell apart in a matter of minutes.

Cronin, who had pinch-hit for Dobson, brought in Bob Klinger for the last of the eighth. Klinger, a journeyman right hander, had not thrown a pitch in the previous six games. Cronin had Earl Johnson, a southpaw, in the bullpen and the leadoff batter for St. Louis in the home half of the eighth was Enos Slaughter, a left-handed hitter.

Slaughter led off the inning with a single. He was still on first base two outs later when Harry Walker, another left-handed batter, came up to hit. He doubled to left-center. Slaughter, who was running with contact because there were two out, scored to give the Cardinals a 4–3 lead.

It was time for Johnson, but by then, it was too late.

The game was not over, though, as the Red Sox tried to fight back. Rudy York and Doerr both singled to open the top of the ninth, and Cronin sent Paul Campbell in to run for York. How slow must York have been? Campbell was, like York, a first baseman who wound up with four stolen bases in 204 major league games and Campbell was, like Klinger, making his first appearance of the entire World Series.

Campbell advanced to third base as Mike Higgins forced Doerr at second, putting the tying run at third with one out. Roy Partee, sent in to catch when Wagner was lifted for a pinch-hitter in the eighth, fouled to first for the second out and Campbell had to stay. Cronin sent in Tom McBride to bat for Johnson and McBride grounded into a force-out to end the inning, the game, and Boston's first World Series in 28 years.

4. Two years later, in 1948, Boston lost the first pennant playoff in American League history, as it would lose the second one 30 years later. Both games were played at Fenway Park.

As agony goes, the '48 playoff loss to the Indians was not very high up on the discomfort scale. When Sox manager Joe McCarthy decided to start 36-year-old Denny Galehouse with his career record of 109–117, the issue was decided. It was 1–1 through three innings, then in the Cleveland fourth, Lou Boudreau and Joe Gordon both singled, then Ken Keltner hit a three-run home run, and the Red Sox were dead.

The loss was not dramatic or agonizing and it was the first time a Red Sox team, or any American League team, had lost that way. What was galling was that Boston had staged a great late-season comeback to get to the playoff. Boston was two games out with four to go and won all four while the Tribe went 2–2. In the playoff, McCarthy erred by giving the ball to Galehouse, but the law of averages was in Cleveland's favor, too—the Indians had not won an American League pennant since 1920.

5. The Sox did not lose the pennant in an official playoff game in 1949, but may as well have. They and the Yankees went into the final game of the regular season with identical records of 96–57. It was a winner-take-all game at Yankee Stadium on October 2, and New York won it, 5–3.

    For a second straight season Boston had performed a near-miracle getting to a point where it could win the pennant. After being swept in a doubleheader by the Athletics—not a bad team that year—on September 11, the Red Sox were three games behind the Yankees with 15 games left to play. Five of those games were against New York; three at Fenway and the final two of the season at Yankee Stadium.

    When New York arrived at Fenway for a three-game series beginning September 24, Boston was two games out of first. When the Yankees left town, the Red Sox were ahead by a game. Going into the final games of the year at Yankee Stadium, Boston was 12–1 in its previous 13 games and needed to win only one of the two in New York to capture the pennant.

    The Yankees won 5–4 and 5–3 and headed for the World Series again.

6. Boston did not make a serious run at the American League pennant again until the Impossible Dream season of 1967 when, as in 1946, it lost the World Series in seven games to the Cardinals. There probably has never been a game of that magnitude played by the Red Sox where the result mattered less than in Game 7 of the '67 World Series. That the Sox were there at all was considered a miracle.

    The Cardinals that year had won 101 games to Boston's 92. St. Louis had clinched the National League pennant early enough to get its pitching in line for the series, while the Sox had to go with their No. 2 starter in Game 1, Jose Santiago, and manager Dick Williams had to gamble in Game 7 by using Jim Lonborg on two days' rest.

The gamble failed as St. Louis won 7–2, but the euphoria of the Sox's regular season achievements did not wear off very quickly. In fact, as sellout crowds populated Fenway Park into the twenty-first century—the miracle never wore off.

7. On August 20, 1972, the Red Sox were one game over .500 in a season truncated by a labor dispute and were apparently going nowhere. Behind the pitching of a rejuvenated Luis Tiant, Boston got hot and went into the final weekend of the season with a chance to win the American League East title. The Sox played the second-place Tigers in Detroit, Boston holding a half-game lead going into a three-game series. It was, essentially, the same kind of best-of-three pennant playoff the National League used to hold.

    The first game of the series was played on October 2, a Monday night, at Tiger Stadium. Detroit scored in the first inning to make it 1–0, but in the top of the third, after pitcher John Curtis struck out leading off the inning, Tommy Harper and Luis Aparicio—two of the best base runners of their generation—connected for consecutive singles. That brought one of the best clutch hitters of his generation, Carl Yastrzemski, to the plate.

    Yastrzemski hit a ball to center field, over outfielder Mickey Stanley's head, more than 400 feet from home plate. Harper scored easily; Aparicio should have, too, but he fell down going around third base. Yastrzemski tore around second base, oblivious to Aparicio's plight, and the teammates wound up on third base together. Yastrzemski was tagged out, and instead of it being a 2–1 Boston lead with a man on third and one out, it was a 1–1 game with Aparicio on third and two out.

    He stayed there and the Sox lost, 4–1. They lost the next night 3–1 and were eliminated. Lost in the lore surrounding Aparicio's stumble, though, was what happened before Boston got to Detroit. The Sox played a Sunday afternoon game in Baltimore and lost to Mike Cuellar and the Orioles, 2–1. It was a very winnable game for Boston, however. Trailing 1–0, the Red Sox had the bases loaded and one out in the fourth and could not score as Carlton Fisk fouled out and Dwight Evans grounded out. After tying the game with a run in the sixth, they had the bases loaded with two out and Doug Griffin flied out. In the top of the ninth, they had runners on first and second with one out and Bob Montgomery, pinch-hitting for Bill Lee, grounded into a game-ending double play.

8. If the Game 7 loss to the Cardinals in the 1967 World Series was almost irrelevant, the Game 7 loss to Cincinnati in 1975 was one of the most relevant and disappointing ones in franchise history. Coming off their riveting victory in Game 6 on home runs by Bernie Carbo then Carlton Fisk, the Red Sox had momentum and perhaps destiny on their side.

   Indeed, the Reds seemed a bit shaken in the early innings. Boston scored three times in the last of the third with the second and third runs coming across when Cincinnati starter Don Gullett walked both Rico Petrocelli and Dwight Evans with the bases loaded.

   Red Sox starter Bill Lee did not treat that lead with care, however. In the top of the sixth, he thought he had thrown an inning-ending double-play ball to Johnny Bench, but second baseman Denny Doyle threw the relay away to keep the inning alive. Bench wound up at second base with two out. Right-handed slugger Tony Perez was up next and the situation cried out for an intentional walk, but Lee tried to get cute and threw Perez an "eephus" pitch—a slow-pitch softball delivery.

   The home run, which reached air traffic control altitude on the way over the Green Monster, cut the Red Sox lead to 3–2. Cincinnati made it 3–3 with a run in its half of the seventh. In the last of the eighth, Boston manager Darrell Johnson sent Cecil Cooper up as a pinch-hitter for reliever Jim Willoughby, who had overpowered the Reds in the top of the eighth, with two out and nobody on base. Cooper fanned to end the inning.

Joe Cronin had pinch-hit for his reliever, Joe Dobson, in a similar situation in Game 7 in 1946, and that strategy worked. It was a similar situation, but not identical. Boston had a runner on first with nobody out in the eighth when Cronin made his move.

With Willoughby out of the game, rookie lefty Jim Burton was brought in and he began the top of the ninth by issuing a walk to Ken Griffey. As always seems to happen, the leadoff walk turned into a run when future-Hall-of-Famer Joe Morgan provided an RBI single, and the run turned into a World Series victory for Cincinnati.

9. The next horrid disappointment for Sox fans was three years away with the team's loss to the Yankees in the second first-place playoff game in American League history, on October 2, 1978, at Fenway Park. That the Red Sox were even playing that game was an example of just how high and low things could get with the Sox. They got to 62–28 at one point in the season and in early July, had a 10-game lead on the second-place Brewers, but saw it all disappear. After the Boston Massacre in early September, when the Yankees swept a four-game series at Fenway, the Sox were tied with the Yanks for first in the AL East and eventually fell 3½ games behind.

And then, magically, they won their final eight games of the regular season to catch up with New York, tie for the division lead, and force the October 2 playoff game.

For all that happened in that game, and there was a lot, especially in the final three innings, its defining moment was Bucky Dent's three-run homer off Mike Torrez in the New York seventh. Legend has it that the home run was a simple fly ball that would have been a fairly routine out in most ballparks, but the homer is on videotape. Anyone who has watched a lot of televised games from Fenway Park can tell by the way the ball leaves a right-handed hitter's bat if it could be trouble, and anyone looking at the ball leaving Dent's bat that afternoon had to be saying "uh-oh."

Dent's home run took the Yankees from a 2–0 deficit to a 3–2 lead, but it was 3–2 in the top of the seventh with two out and nobody on base and still a manageable game for Boston. Things fell apart as Torrez walked Mickey Rivers—as good as a double with Rivers' speed—and after stealing second, Rivers scored the fourth New York run on Thurman Munson's double. Reggie Jackson's homer made it a 5–2 Yankees lead in the eighth, but the Sox battled back with two runs of their own in the bottom of that inning.

The Sox had two runs of their own and runners on first and second with one out, but could not score again. In the ninth, Yankees right fielder Lou Piniella made a miraculous stab of Jerry Remy's base hit with one out and Rick Burleson on first to prevent Burleson from scoring, or at least getting to third base. Boston's season ended with two men on base and Carl Yastrzemski hitting a foul pop-up to New York third baseman Graig Nettles.

10. After the pennant playoff loss to the Yankees, it seemed that things could not get any worse for Sox fans, but they did on October 25, 1986, during Game 6 of the World Series with the Mets, when their team suffered the most excruciating defeat in franchise history, and one of the most agonizing in baseball history.

    One strike away from a World Championship, Boston was beaten 6–5 by the Mets in 10 innings, on a series of two-out singles, a wild pitch, and an error by Bill Buckner. The loss tied the series at 3–3. The Mets won it two days later by beating the Sox 8–5 in a game Boston led by three runs at one point.

11. Losing to the Mets was bad enough, but losing again to the Yankees was another thing entirely, and the last of the post-Ruth sale agonies happened in Yankee Stadium, of all places, on October 16, 2003.

Aaron Boone's home run won Game 7 of the 2003 ALCS 6–5 in the bottom of the 11th, and Jorge Posada's double off Pedro Martinez—Grady Little's fatal error—tied it in the eighth, but the Yankees really won Game 7 in the top of the fourth inning.

Boston was ahead 3–0 going into the top of the fourth and New York starter Roger Clemens was wavering badly. Kevin Millar homered to start the inning, making it 4–0. Clemens walked Trot Nixon, a long-time nemesis, and Bill Mueller followed with a single to center to put runners at first and third with nobody out. The Yankee Stadium crowd watched in stunned silence and dismay knowing full well that one more Red Sox run would almost certainly be it.

With Jason Varitek coming up, Joe Torre lifted Clemens in favor of Mike Mussina, making his first relief appearance after 427 consecutive regular season and playoff starts. Mussina struck out Varitek and induced the speedy Johnny Damon to ground into a double play.

The inning was suddenly over and Boston's 4–0 lead, while formidable, was not insurmountable. Mussina pitched three shutout innings to keep the game manageable. Little's decision to leave Martinez in and Boone's home run kept the Red Sox out of the World Series.

To hear fans who believed in the Curse nonsense talk, one would think that the Red Sox had done nothing but lose and disappoint from the day Ruth was traded to the night they finally won another World Series. But the opposite happened. In reality, Boston played some of the most interesting and exciting baseball in the major leagues after Yawkey bought the club.

As disappointing as the end of the 1948 season was, the Red Sox survived a tremendous three-team race with the Indians and Yankees to even get to the playoff, while across town the Braves were winning the National League pennant. In '49, Boston overcame an awful start and almost miraculously caught New York at season's end. As painful as the final two days of that year were, would it have been better if the Sox had never dug themselves out of their first half hole and just disappeared like the Browns or Athletics?

The long years between 1949 and the 1967 Impossible Dream seemed endless, but 1967 is almost certainly the greatest single season any major league baseball team has ever had, the baseball equivalent of, say, the U.S. gold medal in hockey in the 1980 Olympics, except over a six-month span of time.

Before 2004, I would on occasion do stories about the Red Sox's misfortunes through the years and would ask fans who were around for both the 1986 season and the Impossible Dream, this question: If you had to choose between the Red Sox winning the pennant in 1967 and the Red Sox winning the World Series in 1986—Boston could do one, but not both—which would you pick? It was not unanimous, but about 80 percent of the time, fans would choose to hold on to the Impossible Dream.

The 1975 World Series is still considered a classic, and may be the best one ever played, just as Game 6 may be the best game ever played. Dave Henderson's home run to prolong Game 5 of the 1986 ALCS is one of the most dramatic home runs ever hit, and no franchise has ever experienced a frenzy of winning after changing managers like the Red Sox did during Morgan's Magic in 1988.

Boston teams came back from 2–0 game deficits twice, once against Cleveland and once against Oakland to advance to the ALCS. The Red Sox are the only team to come back from three games down and win a postseason series.

The Curse of the Bambino? An interesting theory, but entirely discredited. Although they didn't know it until Doug Mientkiewicz caught Keith Foulke's underhand toss to end Game 4 of the 2004 World Series in St. Louis, Red Sox fans had it good all along.

CHAPTER 2

THE YANKEES DIDN'T ALWAYS WIN

To hear longtime Red Sox fans talk about their hate-hate relationship with the Yankees, the road from Boston to the Bronx was strictly a one-way street until the momentous fall of 2004.

Okay, the Yankees have been the best franchise in baseball since 1920, when Colonel Jacob Ruppert began using the Red Sox as his team's unofficial Triple A affiliate. The Yankees have won more pennants than the Sox; they've won more World Series than the Sox; and they've won most of the head-to-head battles they've had with the Sox for supremacy in the American League (first) and the American League East (later). Most—but not all.

In fact, when it comes right down to head-to-head battles, Boston has done fine against New York. It's just that the when the Yankees have prevailed it has usually happened in excruciating ways, like the end-of-season matchup in 1949, the Boston Massacre of '78 and the subsequent Bucky Dent playoff game, and Game 7 of the 2003 ALCS.

Boston, however, won the very first two confrontations with New York with first place at stake.

The first one happened in 1904, just one season after the American League had transferred the Baltimore Orioles to New York. Boston, then known simply as the Americans, battled with the New York Highlanders for the AL pennant, with the deciding games played in Manhattan—that's where the team was located before moving across the Harlem

River to Yankee Stadium, and the Manhattan Maulers doesn't have the same ring to it as the Bronx Bombers—on October 10.

Boston and New York were within a half-game of each other, Boston holding the edge after the games of October 5, but the teams had five games left to play against each other, two in Boston and three in New York. On October 7, the Highlanders won at home 3–2 to take a half-game lead in the standings. The next day, at the Huntington Avenue Grounds back in Boston, the Americans swept a doubleheader 13–2 and 1–0 and were back in first place by 1½ games. Both teams had two games left—rainouts and ties were not made up to even off the schedule back then—and they were to be played as a doubleheader in New York on October 10. Boston's magic number was one—the team just had to split the twin bill.

The crowd for the doubleheader was announced at 25,584, a huge gate for those days. The pitching matchup for the first game had Bill Dinneen going for Boston and Jack Chesbro for New York. Chesbro was 41–11, Dinneen was 22–14 and had completed every one of his 36 previous starts that season.

New York scored twice in the fifth inning to take a 2–0 lead, but Boston—shades of 2003 only reversed—picked up two unearned runs in the seventh to make it 2–2, which was the score going into the ninth. In the top of the ninth, catcher Lou Criger led off for the Americans with a single. He was bunted along to second, then moved to third on an infield out. Criger was at third with two out and shortstop Freddy Parent came up.

Chesbro got ahead of Parent 1–0, then threw a wild pitch—did somebody say Bob Stanley?—that allowed Criger to score easily. Parent then singled, but who knows if he would have done that had not Criger scored on the wild pitch. In any case, Dinneen kept the Highlanders from scoring in the bottom of the ninth and Boston had its second-straight American League pennant.

From 1912 through 1918, the Red Sox, as they had finally come to be known, dominated the American League while the New York franchise, by now the Yankees, were annual also-rans. The worm turned after World War I and Boston was so bad for so long that the teams did not go head-to-head for the pennant again until 1948—when for the second straight time it was the Yankees who blinked.

The 1948 American League pennant race was—and still is—one of the league's best ever. Three teams went into the final weekend of the season with a chance to finish in first place—the Indians, who had not won a pennant since 1920; Boston, the '46 AL champs; and New York, the defending American League champions.

On September 30, Cleveland was in first place 1½ games up on both the Yankees and Sox, who had identical records of 94–58. New York and Boston had two games left against each other on October 2 and 3 at Fenway Park. One team had to win both to have a chance to tie the Tribe for first place. A split would eliminate both. The Red Sox got the sweep, beating the Yankees 5–1 behind the pitching of Jack Kramer on Saturday and 10–3 behind Ernie Johnson on Sunday. At the same time, the Indians were losing two out of three to Detroit, and that set up the first pennant playoff in American League history.

Cleveland won the playoff on October 4 at Fenway 8–3, but not before Boston had eliminated New York along the way.

The next time the Red Sox dealt the Yankees chances a fatal blow was in 1959, but it wasn't exactly head-to-head. In '59, Boston was a fading franchise and had switched managers in mid-season, firing Mike Higgins and replacing him with Billy Jurges. It was the season of the Go-Go White Sox and New York was barely hanging on in the pennant race when it came to Fenway Park for a five-game series starting on July 9.

When the series began, the Yankees were 4½ games out of first place and figured to make up some ground against the sorry Sox, who had been bumping along in or near the basement all year long. Instead, Boston swept all five games outscoring New York 50–18 in the process. When it was over, the Yankees were two games under .500 and in fifth place; they were never a factor in the pennant race again.

Here are some highlights of that series.

On July 9, Frank Sullivan hurled a complete game in a 14–3 victory. Vic Wertz and Ted Williams both hit home runs for the Sox. Bobby Avila hit two of the three home runs he had in his entire, although brief, career in Boston. On July 10, Tom Brewer pitched the Red Sox to an 8–5 victory.

On July 11, the teams were tied at 4–4 going into the bottom of the tenth when shortstop Don Buddin, one of the most detested players ever to wear a Boston uniform, hit a grand slam with one out to win it, 8–4. Even better—the Yankees left fielder who watched the ball sail into the screen on top of the Green Monster was Enos Slaughter, whose Game 7 dash around the bases had cost the Red Sox the 1946 World Series.

On the 12th, Massachusetts native Bill Monbouquette threw 6⅓ innings of relief and got the win in a 7–3 victory. Jackie Jensen had the key hit with a three-run homer. And, finally, on July 13, Sullivan worked his second complete game of the series as the Sox cruised, 13–3. Jensen hit another three-run homer and fourth outfielder Gene Stephens, inserted in the game as a pinch runner for Williams in the sixth, hit a grand slam later in the inning.

While the sweep knocked New York out of the pennant race, it did nothing for the Red Sox in that regard. They followed up their mini-massacre by losing 10 of the next 12 games.

In 1975, with the Yankees playing at Shea Stadium, the Sox dealt another death blow to New York's pennant chances by winning three of four from July 25–27, but the Yanks were barely hanging on before that. New York went into the series eight games out and really needed a sweep to recharge its title hopes. The most memorable day of that series was the 27th, when Boston swept a doubleheader, 1–0 behind Bill Lee and 6–0 behind Rogelio Moret. Lee's victory was helped along by an amazing catch center fielder Fred Lynn made in left-center, sliding along the grass as teammate Jim Rice leapt over him to avoid a collision.

In 1988, though, New York had a legitimate chance to catch the Red Sox for first place in the AL East and twice in September, Boston prevailed in head-to-head series. The first one was at Fenway, when they played four games starting September 15. Boston's lead in the division was 4½ games, very similar to the four-game lead it held before the Boston Massacre in '78.

Doom and gloom, panic even, prevailed in New England when the Yanks took the first game of the series, 5–3. In the second game, Boston sent the talented, but unreliable, Wes Gardner to the mound and New York had a 2–0 lead with nobody out and Don Mattingly at first base in the top of the first inning.

Dave Winfield was up for New York. Gardner got him to scald into a double play then struck out Jack Clark to end the inning. Boston came back to win 7–4 then won again the next afternoon 3–1 with Bruce Hurst striking out Clark to end it. The Sox took the fourth game as well, 9–4.

Still, New York had one chance left. The Sox arrived at Yankee Stadium for a three-game series beginning September 23 and led the Bronx Bombers by 4½ games. On the 23rd, a Friday night, New York took a big early lead against Hurst and seemed to be in control. But Boston chipped away against the Yankees bullpen and eventually went ahead 10–9 on Spike Owen's two-run pinch single in the top of the ninth.

The Sox won it 10–9 and as they filed into the clubhouse after the game, veteran reliever Bob Stanley yelled out, "That was a ripper. It ripped the hearts right out of them." Stanley was right. Although Boston lost the Saturday game, Roger Clemens started and Lee Smith finished a 6–0 shutout on Sunday.

The introduction of the Wild Card to the playoff system changed everything about the regular season. Since 1988, it has been mostly about playoff confrontations for New York and Boston. The first two of them went the Yankees' way. The last one, in 2004, made history in that the Red Sox came back from a 3–0 deficit but it was not the first time Boston beat New York head-to-head, and most likely it will not be the last.

THE OTHER BROTHER

Maybe it just seems this way, but don't the Red Sox always wind up with the "other" brother?

While the Yankees were being powered to 10 American League pennants and 9 World Series titles from 1936 to 1951 with Joe DiMaggio on the roster, the Red Sox were winning one pennant and no World Series titles from 1940 to 1953 with Dominic DiMaggio.

Make no mistake about it, Dom DiMaggio was a fine player, a seven-time All-Star and one of the best outfielders in Red Sox history, but Joe is in the Hall of Fame and Dom is not. Joe's career offensive totals were a .325 average, 361 homers, and 1,537 RBIs. Dom's career numbers totaled a .298 average, 87 home runs, and 618

Dominic DiMaggio, left, and his brother Joe DiMaggio, are shown at the All-Star Game on July 8, 1941, in Detroit, Michigan. (AP PHOTO)

RBIs. Both were center fielders and both were great defensive players, but the reality is that Joe was better.

As an example of the way things went into those days, Vince DiMaggio, the third brother, started his major league career with the Boston Braves when they were perennially in the second division.

Then there were the Maddux boys, Greg and Mike. Both arrived in the majors the same year, 1986, even though Mike was five years older than Greg. When Greg retired at the end of the 2008 season, he had 355 wins and four Cy Young Awards. Mike's career record was 39–37.

Greg never pitched for the Red Sox, but Mike did. Boston signed him as a free agent in May of 1995 after he had been released by the Pirates, and Mike went 7–3 in '95 and '96 before being released in the spring of 1997.

The Bells—George and Juan.

George's career lasted from 1981 to 1993 and he spent the majority of it in Toronto, which is where he won the American League Most Valuable Player Award in 1987. George Bell hit 265 home runs and drove in 1,002 runs during his 12-year career, none of which was spent with the Red Sox.

Juan Bell, nine years younger than George, ended his seven-year career by playing 17 games with Boston in 1995. Juan, a utility infielder, had 10 career home runs and 71 RBIs. One of those homers and two of the RBIs came with Boston.

The Royals had third baseman George Brett, who was preceded into the major leagues by six years by brother Ken, a southpaw pitcher. Ken made his debut for the Red Sox in 1967 and actually pitched in the World Series as a teenager. He was 10–15 in four years with Boston and had 14-year career in the majors with 10 different teams, going 83–85.

George played for just the Royals and was in Kansas City for 21 seasons. He hit .390 and was American League MVP in 1980, made the Hall of Fame in 1999, was a .305 lifetime hitter with 317 home runs and 1,595 RBIs, and was a Gold Glove infielder.

Bill Dickey caught for the Yankees from 1928 to 1946, played in eight World Series, hit .313 with 202 home runs and 1,209 RBIs, and was voted into the Hall of Fame in 1954. Bill Dickey's brother, George, was also a major league catcher, and played a little for the Red Sox in 1935 and 1936. George is not in the Baseball Hall of Fame. In 15 games with Boston, George Dickey went 1-for-34.

Finally, the Giambis—and like the Dickeys and DiMaggios, it's a Yankees–Red Sox thing. The Yankees signed Jason Giambi as a free agent after he had spent seven years with Oakland, and as of the end of the 2008 season, Jason was closing in on 400 career home runs.

Jeremy Giambi, three years younger than Jason, was acquired by the Sox from the Phillies in a trade for pitcher Josh Hancock in 2003 and there was some question as to whether Jeremy, or David Ortiz, was the better off-season pickup. Jeremy played in 50 games, hit .197 with 5 home runs, and was released, never to play major league baseball again.

CHAPTER 3

CREDIT WHERE CREDIT IS DUE

For Red Sox fans, it is like the final scene in *Jaws*, where the great white shark is bearing down on Chief Brody and he has one bullet left in the rifle. Will he hit his target, or will the shark chew him up like Captain Quint? No matter how many times you see the movie, you always wonder.

So it is with the video of Dave Roberts' stolen base in the bottom of the ninth inning of Game 4 of the 2004 ALCS. No matter how many times a fan looks at it, there's always that question in the back of his or her mind—is Roberts gonna be safe, or does Jorge Posada get him this time?

Roberts' steal of second just after midnight on October 18, 2004, is one of the defining moments in Red Sox history, and many believe it was the single most important play in their march to a World Series title that October.

It was, indeed, a great moment—unforgettable, critical, crucial, decisive.

But it was not even the most important moment in that inning, let alone that game, that ALCS, or that postseason. The most important moment was Kevin Millar's walk to start the rally in the last of the ninth, and the second most important moment was Bill Mueller's hit to drive in Roberts, who pinch ran for Millar. Without Millar's walk, there would have been no Roberts' stolen base, no Bill Mueller RBI single, no 4–4 tie, no David Ortiz walk-off home run, and no four straight over the Yankees followed by four more over the Cardinals.

You can not re-create the tying run in the ninth without Millar's walk. You can, however, re-create it without Roberts' stolen base, the same way official scorers are allowed to re-create innings to determine unearned runs.

Yankees closer Mariano Rivera walks Millar leading off. Roberts runs for him and is at first base. Those are both givens. But let's say that Roberts doesn't run. Mueller is still the second batter of the inning and Mariano Rivera still has to pay attention to Roberts at first, perhaps even more than if he were at second.

Mueller singles to center. With Roberts' speed and Bernie Williams' arm, Roberts makes third base easily and Boston has men at first and third, nobody out. Doug Mientkiewicz is up next and he bunts. He probably does not squeeze with men at first and third, and even if he strikes out, the Sox still have first and third, one out, for Johnny Damon. Damon then hits a grounder to first baseman Tony Clark, who makes an error, and there's your tying run even without the stolen base.

Of course, it's not that easy, nor was the inning that cut-and-dried. It can stand a much closer look. Millar, for one, loves talking about his part in it.

"I know," he remembered, "that what you hear when people talk about that game is Dave Roberts' stolen base, and Big Papi hitting the walk-off home run. Those are great plays, and none of it happens without the walk but even so, I still think the biggest play of that whole inning was Billy Mueller getting the single.

"That hit is what made everything fall into place. Without that base hit, we're all going home at the end of the night."

The fact that Millar led off that ninth for Boston was a point in the Sox's favor. Rivera was beginning his second inning of work and Millar, although he was prone to striking out, had always been a very tough out for Rivera. He had, however, never walked him.

Millar didn't go up to the plate looking to merely get on base.

Boston's Kevin Millar gestures during a team workout at Fenway Park in Boston, on Thursday, October 14, 2004. The Red Sox would face the New York Yankees the following day in Game 3 of the ALCS series. (AP Photo/Elise Amendola)

"Honestly, I was thinking home run," he said. "And maybe he was thinking about that too, because everything he threw me was up and in so I couldn't get my arms extended."

Rivera threw five pitches to Millar, who took the first one for a ball, then fouled off the second to run the count to 1–1. The next three pitches were similar to the first one, high and inside, and not even close to being strikes.

Manager Terry Francona had Roberts ready to go as a pinch runner if Millar reached and the Sox's reserve outfielder immediately bolted out of the Boston dugout. Roberts was legitimately fast and an excellent base stealer. He was 33-for-34 for the Dodgers before the Red Sox got him via the legendary July 31 deadline trade, but Roberts was a less spectacular 5-for-7 stealing bases in a Boston uniform.

He took a big lead, huge even, off first base, almost daring Rivera to throw over—which is exactly what Rivera did, three times in a row. The third time was almost the charm for the Yankees, and Roberts got his hand back to first base just before the tag applied by Yankees first baseman Tony Clark.

Finally, Rivera went to the plate with a pitch. It was the same pitch he had thrown to Millar three straight times, except with Mueller up batting left handed, it was high and outside, thus a perfect pitch for Posada to make a throw.

The play was close. Roberts was safe at second by about as much, maybe even a little less than he was safe at first, perhaps by a foot. Umpire Joe West was in the right position to make the call and he didn't hesitate with the safe sign, the right sign as it were according to the replay. Mueller ripped Rivera's next pitch up the middle to drive in Roberts with the tying run and the tide of history had begun to change.

In hindsight, it seems simple enough: Walk, pinch runner, stolen base, RBI single. But it was hardly that simple, as Francona remembers.

"I know that everybody who was at that game says they knew (Roberts) was running," Francona said. "Yeah, sure. Now they do. There were a lot of possibilities in that inning, and we talked about a lot of things. We talked about having Mueller bunt. It wasn't our first option, but we talked about it."

When Millar walked, Francona had several things to mull over. The Red Sox had clocked Rivera's time in throwing to home plate, and Posada's time in throwing to second base. "We knew with what the times were that Roberts could steal," Francona said. "And even with that, Posada almost threw him out."

When the Sox looked back and calibrated Posada's throw to second on Roberts' steal, they discovered it was the fastest throw he had ever made in one of their games.

That made the stolen base an attractive possibility, but it still wasn't the only one.

"In Rivera, you've got a guy pitching who doesn't give up a lot of hits," Francona said. "But you've got Mueller up there hitting left-handed, and do you want to give up the hole (with Clark holding the runner)? And Billy had had some success against Rivera."

Mueller actually was 3-for-12 lifetime versus Rivera as he stepped in. Not sensational, but not bad as opposing hitters go against the Yankees stopper. Fresh in everyone's mind, however, were the events of the previous July 24, when Mueller hit a two-run homer off Rivera in the bottom of the ninth to give the Red Sox a dramatic come-from-behind 11–10 victory.

"We talked with (Mueller) about what might happen. We talked with him a lot," Francona said. "We talked about so many possibilities that it looked like he was a little confused when he went up to bat. I'm glad everything happened early in the count."

Why is Roberts' steal of second base the focus of that inning?

Some of it certainly has to do with the fact that the stolen base, for most of Red Sox history, has been a forgotten tool in the team's offensive arsenal. Boston won games with doubles and home runs, not with stolen bases. Some of it may have to do with Roberts himself.

"He is a great, great kid," Francona says. "One of those guys you can't help root for, and when he does have success, you can't help be happy for him."

Millar is like that, too. But lots of Red Sox hitters have gotten bases on balls through the years and lots have been pinch run for. Mueller, the ultimate hero of Boston's ultimate inning, is the opposite of both Millar and Roberts. Mueller was perhaps the quietest regular on the 2004 team of "Idiots," the kind of player who, when he won the 2003 batting crown on the last day of the season in Tampa Bay, sat on a stool in front of his locker with a bucket of iced champagne next to him and talked about his achievement like was ordering a cone of maple walnut ice cream.

Winning a batting title is one thing. Being responsible for the key moment in igniting the greatest postseason comeback in baseball history is another. That's what Bill Mueller did in the wee hours of October 18, 2004, even though most people think it was Dave Roberts.

THE WORST THAT CAN HAPPEN

On March 18, 1953, the Boston Braves announced that they were moving their franchise, a charter member of the National League, to Milwaukee. It was the first relocation by a big-league team in 50 years, or since the American League moved the Baltimore franchise to New York in 1903 and spelled final victory by the Red Sox in a 52-year war for the wallets of Boston's baseball fans.

The battle for the hearts of Boston's baseball fans was over as soon as it began. It just took the Braves a half-century to surrender.

It should have been a triumphant moment for the Red Sox, a chance to capture the loyalty of Braves' fans and create a stronger organization that could once again challenge for the American League pennant. Instead, it was a cue for the Sox to go into hibernation and enter a dreary era of mediocrity that did not end until 1967.

The Braves going to Milwaukee was not the best thing to happen to the Red Sox. It was, at the time, the worst.

From 1876 to 1900, the Boston franchise was one of the jewels of the National League, at least on the field. The predecessors of the Braves, who came upon that nickname in 1912, won pennants in 1877, 1878, 1883, 1891, 1892, 1893, 1897, and 1898. Those teams were also very profitable for the owners, a three-way partnership headed by the penurious Arthur Soden, the inventor of the hideous reserve clause, the contractual swindle that bound a player to his team forever in a comfortable sort of slavery.

Just four seasons after leaving Boston, the Milwaukee Braves found themselves playing the Yankees in the World Series. This is Milwaukee County Stadium during Game 3 of the 1957 World Series. (AP PHOTO)

When the American League was formed in 1901, the Braves had just begun a period of decline, so the Red Sox's timing was impeccable. The new American League franchise built its ballpark on Huntington Avenue, just across the railroad tracks from the Braves' sub-standard South End Grounds on Columbus Avenue.

Having built their ballpark in the small shadow of the South End Grounds, the Red Sox used their National League rivals as a farm team. The Sox raided the Braves' roster for their manager and third baseman, future Hall of Famer Jimmy Collins; first baseman Buck Freeman, who led the 1901 Sox in home runs with 12; center fielder Chick Stahl; and pitcher Ted Lewis, who had won 77 games for the Braves in the previous four years.

The 1901 Red Sox went 79–57, finished second in the American League, and drew 289,448 fans to the Huntington Avenue Grounds. The 1901 Braves went 69–69, finished fifth, and had 146,502 people buy tickets for their games.

And things never really changed.

While the Braves stumbled around the National League's second division, the Red Sox were playing in, and winning, the first World Series. They captured another American League pennant in 1903. Even when the Sox went a horrendous 49–105 in 1906 and finished in last place, they outdrew the Braves. In 1914, when the Miracle Braves went from last place on July 4 to winning the pennant then the World Series, the Red Sox outdrew them, 481,359 to 382,913.

In the entire 52 seasons the teams went head-to-head in Boston, the Braves won the attendance battle just six times—in 1925, 1926, and from 1930-33, after which Tom Yawkey bought the Sox and eventually buried the Braves for good.

Like the Red Sox in the days between Harry Frazee and Yawkey, the Braves were chronically under-capitalized, and that didn't change until the 1940s when construction millionaire Lou Perini bought the team. When World War II ended, the Sox and Braves seemed ready to slug it out on equal footing, but the Braves never had a chance.

The 1946 Red Sox won 104 games and coasted to the American League pennant. The Braves were better than they had been, finished fourth, and were on the way up. In 1948 they won their first National League pennant since 1914, while the Red Sox were beginning their own sort of perverse legend by losing a one-game pennant playoff to the Indians.

The Sox outdrew the Braves by more than 100,000 anyway. The killer, though, was in 1949 when Braves' attendance fell to 1,081,795 and the Sox drew 1,596,650 in a year that ended with another last-day-of-the-season disappointment.

That made it clear. Nothing the Braves could do would change enough minds in Boston to make it a viable National League city. It was time to go and the Braves finally went after drawing 281,278 in 1952 compared to the Sox's 1,115,750 for a team that was two games under .500.

Finally having run their rivals out of town, the Red Sox sat back and did nothing. They were not serious contenders for the American League pennant until 1967. With the Braves gone, the Sox actually drew 90,000 fewer fans to Fenway Park than they did in 1952. Ted Williams' presence kept the team respectable, and kept enough people coming to the ballpark to maintain a viable bottom line.

Meanwhile in Milwaukee, the Braves had blossomed. They received a fabulous welcome in Wisconsin and immediately began setting all-time attendance records—but they were more than a novelty act. The seeds of the Braves' success had been planted in Boston, back when they were trying to find ways to compete with the Red Sox.

The most obvious way was to tap into the tremendous pool of African American talent freed up by the Dodgers' introduction of Jackie Robinson to the major leagues. The Braves signed first baseman George Crowe out of the Negro Leagues in 1949 and sent him to their New England League farm team in Pawtucket. In October of '49 they traded with the Dodgers and got Sam Jethroe, who, along with Robinson, had participated in the farcical tryout at Fenway Park in April of 1945. Jethroe was National League Rookie of the Year in 1950.

In 1952, while still in Boston, the Braves signed Henry Aaron out of the Negro Leagues and sent him to Eau Claire, Wisconsin, to break into pro ball. They also signed African American outfielder Wes Covington, and in short order signed African American outfielder Bill Bruton and Puerto Rican infielder Felix Mantilla.

All the while, the Red Sox remained all white. The team came up with all sorts of excuses, including that all of their farm teams were in the south and they didn't want to subject African American players to abuse, but the Braves put Aaron in Jacksonville, Florida, in 1953 and he excelled, although not without difficulty.

In 1953, the Milwaukee Braves finished second with Bruton and Crowe. Aaron debuted in '54, and by '56 the Braves had Aaron, Covington, Bruton, and Mantilla on the roster. The Braves finished second three times and third once from 1953-56. They won the National League pennant and the World Series in 1957; they won the pennant but lost the World Series in '58; and they finished tied for first with the Dodgers but lost a three-game pennant playoff in '59.

The Red Sox in those years?

They finished 16 games back in 1953, 42 out in '54, and 12, 13, 16, 13, and 19 out in the years 1955–59, respectively. In 1959, they finally brought an African American player up to the majors in utility infielder Pumpsie Green. Pitcher Earl Wilson joined Green later that year and the Sox traded for African American outfielder Willie Tasby in 1960.

How could the Braves leaving Boston for Milwaukee have been the worst thing to happen to the Red Sox?

Had the National League stayed in town, even the Sox in their white complacency would have been forced to keep up. The Braves were in pennant races almost every season after they first moved to Milwaukee, and those empty seats in Braves Field would have filled up quickly in August and September to watch games with the Dodgers and Giants while the Red Sox were playing the Senators to see how high Williams' average could go.

The Braves, with their commitment to signing the best players available no matter what their color or birthplace, would have embarrassed the Red Sox into joining the rest of the modern baseball world and that great, dreary depression in the Fens that lasted from 1951 to 1967 would almost certainly have been shortened by years.

BEN FLOWERS

There is not very much to separate the pitching career of Bennett Flowers from a long list of others who have briefly been in the major leagues, but there is at least one thing.

In 1953, not long after being called up from the minors by the Red Sox to make his big-league debut, Flowers set a major league record by appearing in eight consecutive games. It was a record that stood until Mike Marshall of the Dodgers pitched in 13 straight games in the 1974 season.

The '53 season was the middle year of Lou Boudreau's unsuccessful three-year run as Red Sox manager, and the best year, although the Sox never really were all that close to the first-place Yankees. Flowers, a right-handed pitcher from Wilson, North Carolina, was called up from Triple A Baltimore in June and sent to the bullpen.

In July, as Boston tried to claw its way closer to first place, Boudreau was quoted as saying that, if necessary, "I'll use all of my pitchers every day to win." The manager wasn't just making that up, as Flowers promptly found out.

On July 25, at St. Louis against the Browns, Boudreau brought Flowers into a 7–6 game with two out in the ninth and a runner on base. Flowers faced the dangerous Roy Sievers and got him out to end the game, picking up a save in the process. The next day the Red Sox played a doubleheader, also at St. Louis. Flowers pitched the ninth inning of the first game, stranded two inherited runners, struck out two, and earned another save in a 7–5 Boston victory.

Boston lost the second game 8–5 and Boudreau used Flowers in long relief. He threw four shutout innings, giving up five hits. After a day off, the Red Sox opened a 13-game homestand at Fenway Park and Flowers pitched in each of the first five games, all of them Boston defeats. On July 28, versus the White Sox, he worked one shutout inning in a 4–2 loss; on the 29th he pitched to one batter and got him out in an 8–3 loss. On July 30, Chicago beat Boston 17–1 and Flowers got hit hard like every other Boston pitcher, surrendering nine hits and six earned runs in four innings.

Flowers tied the record of having pitched in seven straight games on July 31 with one shutout inning against the Tigers, who won by a score of 5–3, and he broke the record on August 1 in a game in which he did not officially pitch to anyone.

Skinny Brown started the game for the Sox and was cruising along on the way to an apparent victory when his control deserted him in the ninth inning. Brown started walking people and when he got to a 3–0 count on Detroit catcher Matt Batts, Boudreau ran out of patience and brought in Flowers.

Flowers threw ball four and was relieved. The Sox lost in 10 innings, 5–4. The walk was charged to Brown, and Flowers' line from his record-setting appearance read no innings pitched, runs, hits, walks, strikeouts, or hit by pitch—no nothing. But it counted as a game, and the record was his.

Boudreau gave Flowers the next three days off, then took him out of the bullpen to start a game against the Browns at Fenway Park on August 5. It was the first start of his major-league career and he blanked St. Louis 5–0 on eight hits. The losing pitcher for the Browns was Don Larsen, who, three years later, would throw a perfect game for the Yankees in the World Series.

That was the only game Flowers won in a Boston uniform. He never spent a full season in the major leagues, but did pitch in parts of four different seasons for four different teams.

Traditionally, Flowers has been classified as a knuckleball pitcher, which might account for Boudreau's willingness to use him in eight straight games. Contemporary accounts of Flowers' season in 1953 say, however, that he was actually a pretty hard throwing sidearmer who had control problems at times. Flowers threw a variety of pitches, and the knuckleball was used only occasionally.

For a stretch of eight games in the last week in last week of July 1953, the knuckleball might have been used occasionally, but Flowers was used as often as possible.

CHAPTER 5

BLOODY SOCK

Curt Schilling was a piece of the championship puzzle twice for the Red Sox, both at the beginning of his career when he was traded as a minor leaguer for Mike Boddicker, and the end, when he helped Boston win a World Series. Schilling had a flair for the dramatic and had a flair for getting his name in the headlines and his face on the television screen.

He was unapologetically opinionated, delivering his views on life in general and baseball in particular via his Internet blog, *38 Pitches*. Saying too much can be a dangerous thing for Red Sox players, whose deeds and words are consumed and dissected on a daily basis, and in time Schilling became as much of a target as he was an idol.

Still, he delivered exactly as the Red Sox expected, helping the franchise to two World Series titles in four years after it had won none in the previous 86. But Schilling was such a catalyst for controversy that even his finest hour in Boston was called into question.

The Sox acquired Schilling in November 2003, in a trade with the Diamondbacks. Boston sent pitchers Casey Fossum, Brandon Lyon, and Jorge de la Rosa, and outfielder Michael Goss to the Diamondbacks in exchange for what it thought was the arm and veteran presence that would turn the team from mere contenders into champions. The Red Sox had built an organization that could get to the playoffs most years. Schilling had built a reputation in Arizona, one that was justified by the numbers, as a great playoff performer.

His 2004 regular season performance was tremendous even though he was bothered by nagging, but manageable, soreness in his right ankle caused by a deep bone bruise. Schilling went 21–6 and led the Red

Sox in innings pitched with 226⅔. Schilling didn't help Boston win the AL East title—it was still, back then, the property of the New York Yankees—but he did help the Sox win the American League Wild Card playoff berth.

That matched them up against the AL West champion Angels in the Division Series and Schilling got the ball for Game 1, played in Anaheim on October 5. The Red Sox scored seven runs in the fourth inning and gave Schilling a comfortable early lead, and he protected it well through six good, but not overpowering, innings.

In the sixth, though, Schilling had to cover first base twice on infield grounders, and in the seventh, he had to get off the mound quickly to field Garret Anderson's weak grounder down the first-base line; Schilling was charged with an error on the play and seemed to twist his right ankle as he did it. That's not an uncommon occurrence in baseball, and nobody paid much attention at the time. But Schilling struggled in that inning and had to be taken out; Boston won the game, 9–3, and went on to sweep the Angels, so the twisted ankle was completely forgotten for the moment.

Schilling had six days rest before his next start, which was Game 1 of the ALCS at Yankee Stadium on October 12. As Boston prepared for that game, the ominous news surfaced that Schilling's right ankle was pretty sore, specifically the peroneal tendons. He would get a shot of Marcaine, a pain killer, in the ankle to help him get through the start in the Bronx.

The only thing more numb than Schilling's ankle that night were Red Sox fans as they watched the previously invincible postseason hero get hammered by the Yankees. He lasted only three innings and left with Boston down, 6–0. The score got to 8–0 and the Sox came back to make it 8–7 at one point, but something was obviously wrong with Schilling. One game into the series, Boston was already in trouble.

Schilling had a dislocated peroneal tendon and every time he threw a pitch, he could feel the tendon flopping and popping around in his

Curt Schilling tends to his right ankle during the third inning of Game 6 of the ALCS against the New York Yankees in this file photo taken on Tuesday, October 19, 2004, in New York. The famous bloody sock is now in the Baseball Hall of Fame in Cooperstown, New York. (AP Photo/Charles Krupa)

ankle. Unless the Sox could figure out how to fix it fast, Schilling's postseason was over, and Boston's would be over sooner than hoped.

In what has come to be known as the Schilling Tendon Procedure, Sox orthopedic surgeon Bill Morgan invented a cure. The sheath that kept the tendon in place had torn, which is why it was moving around. So, Morgan used sutures to essentially create a new tunnel for the tendon to move in and prevent it from flopping around.

JASON VARITEK

The morning of August 1, 1997, was one of unrestrained joy for Red Sox fans, and probably for the pitchers in Boston's starting rotation. The day before, Sox general manager Dan Duquette had suckered the Seattle Mariners into taking closer Heathcliff Slocumb in a trade, with Boston getting two minor leaguers in return—pitcher Derek Lowe and catcher Jason Varitek.

Only the most dedicated baseball insiders knew much about either Lowe or Varitek. As far as Sox fans were concerned, getting rid of Slocumb and his blown saves was addition by subtraction. There was no way of knowing then that in the process the Sox had picked up in Varitek a player who would wind up surpassing Carlton Fisk as the team's all-time leader in essentially every catching department.

Varitek was not a sleeper by any means. He was a tremendous college player at Georgia Tech, where one of his teammates was Nomar Garciaparra, and finally signed with Seattle after being its first-round pick in the 1994 draft.

By his own account, Varitek was a terrible defensive catcher when he began his minor league career. Offensively, his bat showed some pop, but he did not hit for average. After Boston acquired him in 1997, he was sent to Triple A Pawtucket where he hit just .197 in 20 games. The Sox made him a September callup and he made his major-league debut on September 24 at Detroit when Jimy Williams used him as a pinch-hitter. Varitek singled and finished the year at 1-for-1.

Boston had not really found a long-term solution at catcher since Carlton Fisk was allowed to go to the White Sox after the 1980 season. For a while, it seemed as though Rich Gedman was the answer, but after collusion left him unsigned at the beginning of the 1987 season, he never recaptured his All-Star form. After that the Sox had the aging Tony Pena, Damon Berryhill, Mike Macfarlane, Mike Stanley, etc.

Varitek began the 1998 season in Boston and split the catching duties with Scott Hatteberg, who could hit for average but was not a great defensive player. In 1999, Hatteberg suffered arm problems and Varitek took over as the No. 1 catcher; Hatteberg didn't get his job back until Varitek suffered a season-ending elbow injury on June 7, 2001. At the end of that season, with Varitek's elbow healed, Boston essentially released Hatteberg.

Jason Varitek holds up the ball after a collision at home plate during Game 3 of the American League baseball championship series against the Tampa Bay Rays in Boston, on Monday, October 13, 2008. (AP Photo/ Winslow Townson)

Throughout his Red Sox career, Varitek has been an offensive enigma. At times, he has hit for power. At times, he has hit for average. In 2004 and 2005 he did both, but as time went on, Varitek's offense suffered, particularly in the latter weeks of a season. His defense, such a concern early in his career, has remained consistently excellent, and his game-calling abilities and his skill in handling a pitching staff are considered to be among the best in the game.

Varitek is such a skilled catcher, that in 2008 he was voted onto the All-Star team by the American League players even though he was batting just .215 at the time of the balloting.

As the 2008 season ended, Varitek was a free agent at the end of a four-year contract. He had caught more games than any other Red Sox catcher

(1,273); had hit more home runs (158), than any other Red Sox catcher; led the franchise list in home runs by a switch hitter (161); and was tied for second with Manny Ramirez on the team's all-time list for postseason homers (11), one behind both Manny Ramirez and David Ortiz.

In Varitek's case, the numbers that mattered most were not batting average or RBIs or home runs. From 1998, when he caught his first game for Boston, through 2008, the Red Sox were 705–468 (.601) when Varitek was the catcher, 256–302 (.459) when he was not.

It's little wonder why he was an All-Star—no matter what his batting average was—and why he joined Carl Yastrzemski and Jim Rice as Red Sox players who were selected as captains.

It had never been done before and nobody knew if it would work. In addition, nobody knew if it would be needed since Boston had lost the first three games of the series and was on the verge of being eliminated. The Sox won Game 4 and Game 5 in Boston, however, to send the ALCS back to Yankee Stadium—Schilling got the start in the sixth game.

He was sensational, shutting down New York for the first six innings while Boston built a 4–0 lead. New York got a run in the seventh but the Sox prevailed 4–1 with Schilling allowing only four hits in seven innings.

Very early in Game 6, a red stain began to appear on the sanitary sock worn on Schilling's right foot. It was right at a line along the top of his shoe and it certainly looked like blood—which it obviously was.

Or not.

Schilling's reputation for the dramatic gesture had grown to a point where there was some suggestion that maybe it wasn't blood after all, that maybe Schilling had put some sort of coloring on the sock to accentuate that his performance was a result of some sort of minor medical miracle.

The theory that the bloody sock was a fake was more of an underground notion throughout that postseason and in the aftermath of

Boston's championship, but it blazed to the forefront early in the 2007 season when Orioles announcer Gary Thorne said during a broadcast in April that backup catcher Doug Mirabelli had admitted that the bloody sock was a fake.

"It was painted. Doug Mirabelli confessed up to it after all. It was all for P.R.," Thorne said on the air.

The next day, however, after talking with Mirabelli, Thorne admitted he had made a mistake. "He said one thing, and I heard something else. I reported what I heard and what I honestly felt was said," Thorne told a group of reporters. "Having talked with him, there's no doubt in my mind that's not what he said, that's not what he meant. He explained that it was in the context of the sarcasm and the jabbing that goes on in the clubhouse. I took it as something serious, and it wasn't."

Mirabelli said that Thorne had gotten it right in his retraction, adding, "He knows that I believe 100 percent that I thought the sock had blood on it. It never crossed my mind that there wasn't blood on that sock. If he misinterpreted something said inside the clubhouse, it's unfortunate."

The surgery made Morgan famous outside of New England and cemented his place in Red Sox history, since Schilling went on to have his ankle sewn up a second time and win a game in the 2004 World Series. Morgan just shakes his head when asked if the blood on Schilling's sock from Game 6 is phony.

"It's ludicrous to think something like that," he said. "To do the procedure, I had to use a really big suture, and they come with really big needles, and the sutures are at the bottom of this hydrostatic pump (Schilling) who weighs about 250 pounds and is pushing hard.

"He's a big guy, pumping hard and he's got this little, white cotton sock on. You know how white cotton absorbs liquid. It could have been four drops of blood, but the stain looks huge. I put a little dressing on it, and actually wanted to put a bigger one on, but Curt said it was bugging him, so we went with the smaller one."

Morgan said he fully expected there would be some relatively minor bleeding when Schilling took to the mound.

"It was real blood," Morgan added, "but it's not like he was bleeding out all over the place. I had to make holes in his skin, and unlike other people, when you do something like that—if it were you or me, we go home and rest. Not him. He was stressing it to the max. It was a big suture, the skin was pushing on it and that would open it up and a little blood would come out."

The Game 6 victory in the ALCS and a win in Game 2 of the World Series at Fenway Park were the apex of Schilling's Red Sox career. Still bothered by the ankle, he missed part of the 2005 season, and wound up in the bullpen as he tried to work his way back to the rotation. Schilling finished the season only 8–8 with a 5.69 ERA. He improved to 15–7 in 2006, but Boston missed the playoffs. In 2007, he battled right shoulder soreness during the summer and was only 9–8; one of the wins was a shutout in Oakland on June 7 in which he was one out away from pitching a no-hitter.

Schilling spent six weeks on the disabled list and returned to pitch well enough, but was obviously getting by on guile and experience, and not pure stuff. Still, he was his usual self in the playoffs, going 3–0 with one win each in the Division Series against the Angels, the ALCS versus the Indians, and the World Series versus the Rockies. His career postseason record for Boston was 6–1 with a 3.28 ERA.

After the 2007 season, Schilling's contract was up. Although he was 41 and coming off a season in which he battled shoulder problems, Boston re-signed him for one more year at $8 million. Even before spring training started, Schilling's shoulder problems surfaced. He and the Sox debated over how to proceed. He wanted immediate surgery; they wanted to wait, figuring that if he had an operation, he was lost to them for good, while a course of rehab and strengthening might get him back later in the year.

It never got him back and he wound up having shoulder surgery. Schilling spent all of his last season with the Sox on the disabled list and did not throw a pitch. Boston wound up paying him $60.5 million for about 3½ seasons worth of pitching, and two World Series titles. The Sox were not complaining, no matter how uneconomical his stay in Boston may have seemed.

Through the perspective of four years and a lot of Red Sox history, Bill Morgan is able to look back on the bloody sock legend and reflect on those dramatic days.

"It was a strange injury for a baseball player, and I would never have done it during the regular season," he said, "but it was the playoffs, and you have a chance to win the World Series, and that made it a totally unique, isolated incident.

"In retrospect, it was a pretty big deal for a multi-million dollar athlete to do something like that, but I'm not surprised that it worked, even though there was no precedent for it. It was a 'feel' kind of thing, one of those things that experience tells you you can take for granted. I knew it would work for what we wanted then."

The Sox wanted their first world championship in 86 years and they got it, thanks in large part to Schilling and his right sock from Game 6 of the 2004 ALCS. It wound up in the Hall of Fame, and was definitely Schilling's sock, and it definitely had Schilling's blood on it.

BILL BUCKNER

Most managers get fired simply because somebody's got to take the blame when things go wrong and it is easier to pin the tail on one donkey than 25 of them. Think of Herbert Hoover and the Great Depression, an economic calamity a decade in the making.

This explains why Bill Buckner unjustly has come to symbolize the entire horrifying night of October 25, 1986. Buckner's error that evening at Shea Stadium didn't cost the Red Sox Game 6 of that World Series against the Mets, and he has a right to be bitter about his role as some sort of villain in the defeat. He was just one of several contributors to that disaster.

Gene Mauch, who managed the Angels team that Boston beat to reach the '86 World Series, argued with umpires but never blamed them when his team lost. While umps might make bad calls, Mauch reasoned, over the course of a nine-inning game a team can always do something to remedy its misfortune.

Throughout Game 6 the Red Sox had countless chances to remedy Buckner's mistake, mostly by doing things early in the game that would have made it meaningless. On that night in Queens, Boston batters left 14 men on base, seven of them in scoring position. Buckner himself left the bases loaded to end the eighth.

There are other key points where that game could have turned, and Jim Rice was involved in two of them. In the first, Rice was on first base with two out when Dwight Evans hit a double off the fence. That should have been a run, but Rice only made it to third base. In the

Bill Buckner is a picture of dejection as he leaves the field after committing an error on a ball hit by New York Met Mookie Wilson which allowed the winning run to score in the sixth game of the World Series on Saturday, October 25, 1986, in New York. (AP Photo/Rusty Kennedy)

seventh, Rice was at second with two out when Rich Gedman singled; Rice was thrown out at home by Mookie Wilson.

In the fateful last of the tenth, a zillion things happened. Sox pitchers kept getting two strikes on Mets batters, but not getting them out; there was the Bob Stanley wild pitch; there was John McNamara's decision to not get Calvin Schiraldi out sooner; and his decision to have Buckner and not Dave Stapleton at first base. Who is to say Stapleton would have made the play on Wilson's ground ball? Buckner could not run well, but that had nothing to do with the way he played Wilson's grounder. It was one of those weird, spinning balls that looked like trouble the second it left the bat.

Before that, there was the pitching change that got Roger Clemens out of the game in place of Schiraldi, and both sides—McNamara and

Clemens—have had opposing stories. The manager said Clemens asked to be taken out. Clemens said he did not. For what it's worth, Bill Fischer—the Boston pitching coach at the time and Clemens' mentor—has steadfastly refused to talk about what happened that night, even to close friends, and that tends to support McNamara's side of the story.

Even after that, Boston had a chance to remedy what happened in Game 6 by winning Game 7, and at one point in that game, the Sox had a 3–0 lead before losing, 8–5.

For that matter, the 1986 World Series didn't even have to get to a Game 6. The Red Sox beat the highly favored Mets in the first two games, both played at Shea Stadium. Since the first World Series was played in 1903, only one team had ever won the first two games of a World Series on the road and then lost the series. That had happened just the year before, in 1985 when the Cardinals won the first two games in Kansas City but lost the series in seven.

Boston headed to Fenway Park with 2–0 lead on the Mets, and had gone 51–30 at home during the regular season. It could be said that the '86 World Series was actually lost in the first at-bat of Game 3 at Fenway Park when Lenny Dykstra hit a dinky home run down the right-field line off Oil Can Boyd. That led to a four-run first inning and momentum-changing 7–1 victory for the Mets.

The Red Sox's pitching failed again in Game 4 at Fenway and New York won 6–2, ensuring that the series would return to Shea Stadium. If Boston had finished off the Mets in four or five games, the Game 6 disaster would never have happened. An ounce of prevention, etc.

For some unfathomable reason, baseball games, series, and seasons seem to acquire lives of their own and nothing that mere mortals can do will change that. On the final day of the 1967 season, when the Red Sox beat the Twins at Fenway Park to clinch at least a tie for first place, they rallied for five runs in the sixth inning after starting that inning with four straight hits. Two of them, ground balls by Jerry Adair and Dalton Jones, were a couple of feet away from being rally-killing double plays, but the comeback's success seemed to be predetermined.

And in 1986, was there ever a question in anyone's mind that after Boston came back from the dead to beat the Angels in Game 5 in Anaheim the Sox would win Games 6 and 7 and take the series? So it was in Shea Stadium on the night of October 25, 1986. Once the Mets tied that game they were bound to win it and the World Series.

When Buckner returned in 2008 to throw out the first pitch at the Red Sox's home opener where they received their 2007 World Series rings, he was greeted warmly by the fans in what was characterized as an all-is-forgiven atmosphere. Boston fans, though, had forgiven Buckner immediately after 1986. He was at Fenway for the home opener in '87 and was received, if not warmly, then without malice. In 1990, he was a spring training invitee and made the team as a bench player, and was cheered warmly when he was introduced at the Fenway opener that year.

So, when in 2008 he blamed the media for perpetuating the myth about him being responsible for Boston's World Series defeat in 1986, Buckner had a valid point. After the pregame ceremony where he threw out the first ball, Buckner spoke emotionally about the aftermath of Game 6 and what it meant in his life.

"I really had to forgive," he said, "not the fans of Boston per se, but I would have to say, in my heart, I had to forgive the media...for what they put me and my family through. So, I've done that, and I'm over that. And I am just happy that I try to think of the positive, the happy things.

"You can look at that series and point fingers in a whole bunch of different directions. We did the best we could to win, and it just didn't happen, and I didn't feel I deserved so much blame. It was a great season. There's a lot of good memories and I'm just happy I can focus on those."

Buckner is right. He never deserved the abuse he has received. Nor has Steve Bartman, the unfortunate Cubs fan at Wrigley Field in 2003. Nor Denny Galehouse in 1948. Baseball is far too complex a sport—and that's the basis of its appeal, no?—for one play to have decided the outcome of any one game.

In 1986, Buckner happened to have the handiest tail to pin the blame on.

CHAPTER 7

THE RED SEAT

Time plays tricks with the memory, and those who live in the present are quick to dismiss legends of the past as fantasies or exaggerations. So it has become with a single seat in the Fenway Park bleachers—Section 42, Row 37, Seat 21—The Red Seat, where 56-year-old Joseph Boucher was sitting on June 9, 1946, the day he was struck on top of the head by a baseball hit by Ted Williams.

A lot has changed at Fenway Park since that summer afternoon. The bleachers where Boucher sat were true bleachers, long wooden benches with no protection from the sun. Through the years, Fenway Park was modernized and along the way the bleachers were gentrified, and relatively comfortable plastic seats took the place of the splintery wooden benches.

So the Red Seat is a relatively new addition to the Red Sox scene, and as a matter of fact, it is probably not *exactly* in the right place, although it is in the neighborhood.

Williams' blast is considered to be the longest home run ever hit at Fenway Park and one of the longest in baseball history. It is also considered by most Red Sox players who have gazed out in that direction to be a fairy tale. "It is a myth. A myth," former Boston first baseman Mo Vaughn said whenever asked about the Red Seat. "No man can hit a baseball that far."

"I went out and stood at that seat," said former Sox right fielder Trot Nixon. "And nothing against Ted Williams, but I don't see how anyone could hit a ball that far. I've never seen a ball come close, not even in batting practice, and there have been some great hitters here over the years."

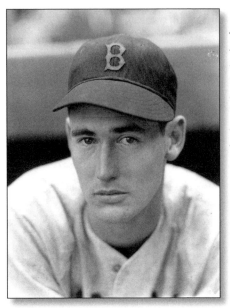

Ted Williams "The Splendid Splinter" on May 23, 1941. Five years after this photo was taken, Williams would be back with the Red Sox after serving in the military during World War II and would hit the longest home run in Red Sox history. (AP PHOTO)

Sox broadcaster Jerry Remy has always been skeptical, too. "I've never seen anybody come close to it," said Remy. "The longest ball I've ever seen hit here was by Eddie Murray, and he hit it to the runway in center field, the one back behind the bullpen, and that's not nearly as high as where the red seat is. I remember, as a player, seeing home runs hit out there and saying to myself, 'Whoa' —and as a player, you don't have that reaction very often—and those home runs land maybe five rows over the bullpens."

The Red Sox media guide lists the red seat as being 502 feet from home plate. Former Sox manager Joe Morgan, during his tenure in the Rectangular Office, once measured it at 519 feet. It looks closer to 519 than 502, and it is. The distance was measured for a newspaper story and, while not done as precisely as a surveyor might do it, was performed carefully and has the seat at about 514 feet from the plate.

The spot where the ball hit Mr. Boucher's head was measured at about 33 feet above field level. So, in comparison, a right-handed hitter's equivalent of the Red Sox blast would be with the Green Monster moved back 200 feet from its present site, with the ball hitting four feet from the top of it.

If Sox players only familiar with the modernized Fenway Park are disbelievers, longtime player, coach, and manager Johnny Pesky played in the game and does believe. "Actually, what I remember most is the sound," he said. "The crack of the bat sounded like a cannon shot. And the ball took off the way a rocket does, and just carried and carried."

The Tigers pitcher that day was Fred Hutchinson. "Hutchinson was a breaking-ball pitcher," Pesky said. "He threw just hard enough to set up his breaking ball."

In a 1996 interview with Dan Shaughnessy of the *Boston Globe*, Williams said he hit a changeup. Williams had a Hall of Fame memory, especially when it came to hitting, and it seems safe to say that Hutchinson threw him a changeup.

There were six daily newspapers in Boston in 1946 and all of them covered the game. Five of those papers gave detailed descriptions of the home run, but there were some differences in their accounts.

According to the *Boston Herald*, the ball landed about halfway up the bleachers. That paper estimated the distance at 500 feet. The *Boston Post's* account had the ball landing about two-thirds of the way up, but said the bleachers contained 60 rows, when there actually are slightly fewer than 50. The tabloid *Boston Record* described it as the longest home run ever seen at Fenway and guessed that it landed between 25 and 30 rows up; so did the *Boston American*.

The *Boston Globe* provided the most detailed description of The Red Seat shot. Reporter Harold Kaese was the only one who interviewed Boucher, and he said, "The sun was right in our eyes. All we could do is duck. I'm glad I didn't stand up. They say it bounced a dozen rows higher, but after it hit my head, I was no longer interested."

Kaese identified Boucher's seat as being in Section 42, Row 33, directly next to the aisle and said it was a bit more than halfway up the bleachers. That is different from where the Red Sox have located The

Red Seat—a cause for some confusion, and an issue that will be dealt with in a bit. Oddly, even though Kaese had the most exact placement of where the ball landed, his estimate had it going only 450 feet.

While there were no photographs of the home run itself, there is one legendary picture of Mr. Boucher and his hat. That photo shows a hole directly in the middle of the top of the straw hat, a clue that the ball was descending almost straight down when its trajectory intersected with Mr. Boucher's scalp.

There were also two cartoonists at the game. The *Globe* cartoon showed the ball landing just above the runway behind the bullpen. The *Post* cartoon had it coming to earth at almost the exact spot The Red Seat is at today, perhaps a bit lower. So by all accounts, Williams' home run was an exceptional one, and unquestionably the longest one ever hit to that part of the ballpark. But did it really go that far, or is it, as Vaughn contended, a myth?

The most likely answer seems to be that The Red Seat is not a myth, but is probably a slight exaggeration, and a lot of what happened and how has to do with the weather on that early June afternoon.

The day before, New England was pummeled by a weather system that produced, among other things, vicious hailstorms. As the storms moved out to sea, a contrasting system of very dry air moved in. As usually happens, the change in air produced a fierce prevailing wind. That afternoon, the weather at Fenway Park included an unusually strong 20-mph tailwind with temperatures in the mid-70s and very low humidity. That made it a perfect day to hit.

It was perfect enough so that Red Sox center fielder Dom DiMaggio, a right-handed batter who was only 5'9" and weighed 168 pounds, and who hit just four home runs at Fenway Park in that entire 1946 season, hit one into what is now the Boston bullpen.

To take a more scientific look at The Red Seat homer, two assistant professors of physics at the College of the Holy Cross in Worcester, and baseball fans both—Matthew Koss and Timothy Roach—looked at the numbers. They created a spreadsheet and ran different possibilities and came up with this theory, "The best bet is that Ted Williams pulled a changeup into a 20-mph tailwind at a launch angle of 30 to 35 degrees and at 117-118 mph. Therefore, if the ball were allowed to continue from where it landed in the seats, it would have gone an additional 28 to 34 feet for a total of 542 to 548 feet from home plate."

Some studies on the physics of baseball indicate that 550 feet is probably the far edge of how far a ball can be hit, and 120 mph is probably the far edge of how fast a batted ball can travel. Given all that, Williams' colossal home run is at the far edge of possibility but a possibility, nonetheless.

"I have to say that it can't be ruled out," Koss reported. He was troubled by the fact that Williams hit a changeup, meaning that the speed of the pitched ball didn't give Williams much help. What probably made the remarkable distance of The Red Seat home run possible was the wind. It had a huge effect. In fact, on a day with no wind, DiMaggio's home run for instance would have traveled 50 feet less and been just an easy out in right-center.

So, it would appear that The Red Seat homer was the Fenway equivalent of The Blizzard of '78, The Perfect Storm, the USA's hockey gold medal in 1980, or even Bob Beamon's record-shattering long jump in the 1968 Olympics—a once-a-century confluence of all sorts of favorable factors that produced unimaginable results.

There remains the nagging question of how The Red Seat came to be in Row 37, Seat 21. Nobody seems to know. The Fenway bleachers were remodeled 20 years ago, and the wooden benches that Mr. Boucher sat on were replaced by individual seats. But the 30-inch-wide concrete steps that the seats were bolted to have not changed. There is the same number of rows in 2003 as there was in 1946. However, in the remodeled bleachers, there is a wide walkway at the bottom to provide space for handicapped access. The first row of actual seats is Row 3. If in 1946 it was Row 1, then that accounts for part of the difference.

If measurements are made from the seat closest to the aisle on Row 33, not 37, guess what? The distance comes to 502½ feet from home plate, almost exactly what the Red Sox say is how far Williams' home run traveled. Putting The Red Seat there, according to Koss and Roach's figures, would have the home run going a maximum distance of 526 to 532 feet, a much more believable figure.

There is one more piece of convincing evidence for Williams having been able to hit a ball that far and it was provided by his successor in left field, Carl Yastrzemski, in 1977. For the Red Sox, that was a year of home runs. They hit 213 homers as a team; on July 4 at Fenway, they hit eight home runs against the Blue Jays. The ball was traveling well that summer.

On June 19, 1977, Boston played the Yankees in a Sunday afternoon game at Fenway Park and won, 11–1. The Red Sox hit five home runs in the game and with one out in the eighth, Jim Rice and Yastrzemski hit back-to-back home runs off reliever Dick Tidrow. Yastrzemski's soared high over the right-field foul pole hit the facing of the roof over the grandstand in the right-field corner.

It was the first time anyone watching the game had ever seen a ball hit the facing of that roof. It is mentioned in all the accounts of that game; the Red Sox own a video clip—not great quality, but a clip—of the ball striking the facing of the roof. So, it happened. There can be no memories playing tricks regarding the Yastrzemski blast that day.

The Yankees right fielder was Reggie Jackson, who told reporters after the game, "It missed going out by two inches."

The facing of the right-field roof is directly over the 20th row back from the right-field corner. That puts it 60 feet from the low fence in that corner, at a spot about 365 feet from home plate. Yastrzemski's home run hit the facing of the roof about 425 feet from the plate, and the roof there is about 40 feet about the level of the playing field. The video footage isn't clear enough to show the trajectory of Yastrzemski's homer as it hit the facing of the roof, so there is no way of knowing if it was headed straight down or still had some forward momentum.

Newspaper accounts of the blast say it was still rising, which is preposterous, but that does indicate it wasn't dropping straight down.

Whatever the math, nobody before or after has hit a ball that far to that part of Fenway. If that can be done, the likelihood that Williams' home run traveled more than 500 feet seems more plausible.

That today's players can't imagine such home runs and have seen nothing come close is not necessarily surprising. The construction of what was then called the 600 Club in 1989 changed wind conditions at Fenway Park, and in particular cut down on the summer winds that blew in from behind home plate. That change in the tailwind factor could account for why none of today's Red Sox hitters can come close to The Red Seat no matter what the weather.

The Bible of home runs is *The Home Run Encyclopedia*, edited by Bob McConnell and David Vincent and published by the Society of American Baseball Research in 1996. In that book, researcher William J. Jenkinson concludes that most of the legendary long home runs of the past are exaggerations. A prime example is Mickey Mantle's famous home run in Washington, D.C., in 1953. It was reported to have traveled 565 feet, but that was the distance where the ball was retrieved, not where it landed. It hit the earth at about 510 feet then bounced and rolled.

At the Row 37 placement, Williams' home run may indeed be the longest in the history of baseball. Even at Row 33, which seems to be a minimum distance, it remains one of the most epic blasts in the history of the game. And while players who have come and gone since then shook their heads in disbelief as they gazed at the tiny red dot in the right-field bleachers, and as today's players do, one thing has to be remembered.

Ted Williams is the man who, on the last day of the 1941 season, went into a doubleheader hitting .396 and rather than protecting his average, played two games and went 6-for-8 to finish at .406. He is the same man who, also in 1946 at Fenway, became the only player ever to hit a home run off of Rip Sewell's eephus pitch, a softball toss that may have been thrown at something like 50 mph maximum. He is also the same man who, at age 39 in 1957, batted .388 and the same man who, on a cold, damp, dreary late September day in 1960—the kind of day when nobody can hit a home run to right field at Fenway Park—took the last swing of his life and put a ball into the Red Sox bullpen.

The Red Seat?

While it has become a legend, it is not a myth and has never been one. It may not be in exactly the right place in the bleachers, but it can never lose its place in Red Sox history.

CHAPTER 8

THE TURNING POINT

While reality never changes, perception does, so pinpointing the most important date in Red Sox history becomes a matter of perspective.

Was it October 27, 2004, when Boston beat the Cardinals in St. Louis to win its first World Series in 86 years? Or maybe just a week earlier, on October 20, when it capped an unprecedented comeback by beating the Yankees in Yankee Stadium in Game 7 of the ALCS?

It could be February 26, 2002, when the ownership group of John Henry, Larry Lucchino, and Tom Werner ended 69 years dismal years of Red Sox history by passing final papers on the purchase of the franchise from the Yawkey Estate.

How about October 1, 1967, when the Impossible Dream came true with a 5–3 victory over the Twins at Fenway Park? April 20, 1939—Ted Williams' first appearance in the major leagues? April 20, 1912—the day Fenway Park officially opened for business?

Perhaps even April 26, 1901, when Boston went to Baltimore and played its first-ever game as a member of the American League?

All good answers, but all are incorrect. The most important date in the long history of the Boston Red Sox is September 16, 1965, when owner Tom Yawkey finally put an end to the "isms" that had powered his team—racism, alcoholism, cronyism—since he purchased it in 1933. On that afternoon, while Dave Morehead was throwing a no-hitter at the Cleveland Indians, Yawkey fired general manager Mike Higgins and replaced him with Dick O'Connell.

When Yawkey finally acted, his Red Sox had reached the lowest point of his ownership. Morehead's no-hitter gave Boston a 58–91 record in a season that would finish 62–100, the worst record of Yawkey's ownership. Attendance at the game was 1,247; attendance for the season was 652,201, the lowest since 1945. The Boston lineup for the game that day included eight all USA-born white players, and Puerto Rican Felix Mantilla, the one minority.

Yawkey bought the Red Sox in 1933, and when he decided to make the purchase, it was contingent on Eddie Collins, the future Hall of Fame infielder, joining him as general manager. From '33 until the day he fired Higgins, Yawkey had ex-players as GMs—Collins, Joe Cronin, Bucky Harris, and finally Higgins.

O'Connell was different. He was not a former player. He had no old clubhouse friends to reward with jobs, no cronies to take care of. O'Connell took over as general manager with a clean blackboard and an open mind. He was a graduate of Boston College and had stumbled into professional baseball almost accidentally, having met Sox broadcaster Jim Britt in the navy during World War II.

O'Connell quickly went from running the Sox's minor league team in Lynn to being part of the management team at Fenway, but his responsibilities were restricted to the business side. Cronin was the GM and under him the Red Sox remained the whitest team in baseball. Higgins had two tours of duty as a Red Sox player and became the manager of Boston's Class B farm team in Roanoke, Virginia, after retiring at end of the 1946 season. He moved up the managerial ladder and took over in Boston in 1955.

Cronin remained as general manager until he was hired as American League president in 1959. Harris, at the end of the line, was GM for just two years. The Sox did not officially have a general manager, in 1961 and '62. O'Connell handled the business affairs and Higgins managed and took care of player personnel moves. Finally, after another second-division finish in 1962, Higgins was promoted, which is how things worked in those days for the Red Sox.

On March 17, 1964, Red Sox executive vice president Dick O'Connell (right) announced that the proceeds from the home-opener would be donated to the John F. Kennedy Memorial library in Boston. O'Connell is talking to Senator Edward M. Kennedy, D-Mass. (AP PHOTO/BILL CHAPLIS)

The first game of O'Connell's tenure was Morehead's no-hitter. Higgins was fired around noon, but stuck around long enough to have a drink and pregame meal in the press dining room before heading out of the ballpark and into the dustbin of Red Sox history.

The first thing O'Connell said as new general manager was that he wasn't smart enough to make player moves by himself. "We will endeavor to get someone to have active charge of player personnel," he said. "A person outside the Red Sox organization who may have some new ideas."

And there it was—the business as usual days were gone.

RAY CULP

When you think Red Sox and the best trades the team has ever made, you probably think of names like Pedro Martinez, Jackie Jensen, Derek Lowe, and Jason Varitek.

It is typical of Ray Culp that the trade that brought him to Boston is overshadowed by other deals involving bigger names, but it was one of the best in Red Sox history, just as he is one of the best pitchers to ever wear a Boston uniform.

Dick O'Connell acquired Culp from the Cubs on November 30, 1967, in exchange for Bill Schlesinger and some money. Culp had pitched for the Phillies for four pretty good years before going to the Cubs, where he was an unspectacular 8–11 in 1967. Schlesinger's Red Sox career, and as it turned out his entire major league career, consisted of one at-bat in the sixth inning of a game against the Angels on May 4, 1965.

He pinch-hit for pitcher Dave Morehead and grounded back to the pitcher. End of career.

At first, it looked like the Cubs got the best of the deal. In Culp's first start for Boston, he gave up 8 runs in $3\frac{2}{3}$ innings. The next time out, it was 5 runs in $2\frac{2}{3}$ innings. It wasn't until the middle of May that he pitched well enough to earn a regular spot in the rotation, but when he finally did, Culp was superb.

In the season's second half, he was better than superb. He put together one of the best stretches of starting pitching in team history, beginning on July 29, when he beat the Orioles at Fenway 3–2 with a 10-inning complete game. A month later, Culp progressed from being good to being historic by pitching seven complete games in a row, including four straight shutouts.

On August 27, he beat the Indians 7–1 with a complete game. On September 1, it was a 7–4 win over Washington; on the 7th, a 2–1 win over the Angels; on the 13th, a 3–0 shutout of the Twins; the 17th, a 2–0 shutout of Baltimore; the 21st, a 2–0 victory over the Yankees; and the 25th, a 1–0 blanking of Washington. The game against New York was a one-hitter, the only hit was Roy White's single with two out in the seventh.

His scoreless streak during that September run of complete games reached 39 innings. Culp finished the season 16–6, but 1968 was the Year of the Pitcher, and his scoreless streak was only the fourth best in baseball that season.

As it turned out, Culp's success had nothing to do with the height of the mound. He was 17–8 in 1969 and 17–14 in 1970, a year in which his ERA was 3.04 and he threw 15 complete games.

Culp battled shoulder soreness throughout his career, and midway through the 1972 season he had to stop pitching. The initial diagnosis was calcium deposits. Surgery later revealed a torn tendon, and his career was essentially over. A year later Culp tried it again, but was able to make only nine starts before the pain got to be too much.

Culp grew up in Austin, Texas—where he became successful in real estate after his career ended—and he wore No. 21 with the Red Sox. His 71 wins are third among Boston pitchers who had 21 on their back behind two other Texans—Roger Clemens and Tex Hughson. Clemens pitched for four Red Sox teams who made it to the postseason and Hughson won 20 games for the 1946 pennant winners. Culp's teams were good, but not contenders, which is probably why his career, and the trade that brought him to Boston, don't get the kind of recognition they deserve.

The man O'Connell hired to be in charge of player personnel turned out to be Haywood Sullivan, who had spent most of his playing career with the Red Sox but was managing the Kansas City Athletics when O'Connell called. Eventually, O'Connell was able to figure out the player personnel side of things and Sullivan was relegated to running the scouting department. Later, Sullivan took O'Connell's job and became part of ownership.

The Red Sox transformation from being one of baseball's dinosaur franchises to being one of its crown jewels occurred astoundingly fast. When O'Connell took over as GM, no Boston team had even been in contention for first place in September since 1951; the Red Sox won the American League pennant in '67; missed the AL East title by a half-game in '72; and went to the World Series in '75.

The team that O'Connell took over drew 1.5 million fans for the two previous seasons combined. The 1967 Sox drew 1.7 million, and the team led the league in attendance in seven of the next nine years. Aside from the '66 team, none of O'Connell's clubs finished below .500, and starting in '67, Boston won more games than it lost for 16 straight years—long after he was fired.

O'Connell inherited a manager, the laidback, disconnected Billy Herman, who was under contract through 1966. He let Herman stay into September of '66 and then, even though the Sox had shown improvement after the All-Star break, fired him with 16 games left in the year. O'Connell replaced Herman with the irascible, edgy, hard-driving Dick Williams, the type of manager the team had not had since Ed Barrow, whose Sox won the 1918 World Series.

It took a while for O'Connell to get his feet under him, although he got busy early. His first deal as GM was to trade local hero Bill Monbouquette to the Tigers for George Thomas and George Smith. Thomas was a good utility man for five years. He then purchased right-handed pitcher Jose Santiago from Kansas City. Santiago started Game 1 of the 1967 World Series. In December 1965, O'Connell dealt Lee Thomas, a Higgins acquisition, and erratic southpaw Arnold Earley to the Braves for Bob Sadowski and Dan Osinski. Osinski helped win the pennant in '67.

It wasn't until June 1966 that O'Connell got serious about re-making the Red Sox, and when he did, he was fearless about it. On June 2, he traded Dick Radatz, the best reliever in Red Sox history, to the Indians for pitchers Don McMahon and Lee Stange. On the 13th, he made a six-player deal with the Athletics and got John Wyatt and Jose Tartabull, both key men in '67, as part of it. The next day O'Connell sent the Sox's best starter, Earl Wilson, to the Tigers for outfielder Don Demeter.

When Williams whipped the Red Sox into contention in the early months of 1967, O'Connell responded with more wheeling and dealing. He used McMahon as bait in a trade with the White Sox that brought over Jerry Adair. He sent Demeter to the Indians for Gary Bell. He bought Norm Siebern from the Giants, got the aging Elston Howard from the Yankees essentially for nothing, and paid Ken Harrelson $150,000 when Charlie Finley made him a free agent at the end of August.

Meanwhile, O'Connell set about to restock Boston's farm system. For years the Sox had scouted and signed offense, offense, offense. The frontline players who came up through the farm system could hit but could not run, and with the rare exception of a Frank Malzone were desultory defensive players.

From 1960–65, Boston developed only four pitchers who had any impact at all and one of them was Wilbur Wood, whose success came as a knuckleballer with the White Sox. Don Schwall was Rookie of the Year in 1961 but quickly faded; Dave Morehead pitched the no-hitter on the day O'Connell was hired, but was 35–56 lifetime with the Red Sox. That left Radatz and Jim Lonborg as the only truly significant pitchers developed by Boston in the years immediately prior to O'Connell taking over.

O'Connell became general manager just as baseball implemented the amateur free-agent draft and the Red Sox soon created one of the deepest farm systems in the game. His scouts drafted Ken Brett, Bill Lee, Carlton Fisk, Ben Oglivie, Cecil Cooper, Rick Miller, Rick Burleson, Dwight Evans, Jim Rice, Fred Lynn, Butch Hobson, Bob Stanley, Don Aase, John Tudor, Bruce Hurst, Glenn Hoffman, and Wade Boggs.

As a trader, O'Connell consistently made bold moves. He got Ray Culp for nothing. He dealt the immensely popular Harrelson to Cleveland in April 1969, right after Harrelson had established "The Hawk" persona. O'Connell traded away Tony Conigliaro after his sensational comeback season of 1969—36 homers, 116 RBIs—and Conigliaro never approached those numbers again.

O'Connell signed Orlando Cepeda to be Boston's first designated hitter and Cepeda was the perfect man for the job. He took a chance on Luis Tiant. He fired Dick Williams less than two years after the

Impossible Dream and fired Darrell Johnson the year after the 1975 World Series. He traded Sparky Lyle for Danny Cater; traded Lonborg and George Scott; essentially gave away Oglivie and Cooper.

O'Connell was not perfect, but he was a different voice in an organization that had become complacent with unimaginative consistency. Red Sox history did not start with the hiring of Dick O'Connell as general manager, but the history of capacity crowds, playoff series, innovative thinking, and "Red Sox Nation" as it has come to be known—all started with Dick O'Connell.

CHAPTER 9

MORGAN'S MAGIC

By the time the Red Sox finally let manager John McNamara go, it amounted to a mercy firing. Fans had never forgiven him for what happened in the 1986 World Series, and after that defeat Boston played sub-.500 baseball.

In 1988, ownership let McNamara stew about his future through the All-Star break, and had gone so far as to actually let him drive into Fenway Park on July 14, and fill out a lineup card for that night's scheduled game with the Royals. There are two doors to the manager's office at Fenway Park—one that leads into the clubhouse, and a side door that opens onto the corridor that leads to the players' parking lot. About three hours before game time, the door to the clubhouse closed and the side door opened for Gorman and minority owner Haywood Sullivan, McNamara's friend. And with that, Mac was gone.

The press conference and formal announcement came a bit later. The way that many found out about it was by simply looking at the door that opened into the clubhouse. The name on it—"McNamara"—had been clumsily covered over by black electrical tape, like a sheet drawn over a body, with the outline of the name underneath still quite obvious. Below it, in equally clumsy fashion, a few magnetic letters had been stuck to the door in the form of "Morgan."

When the Red Sox hired Joe Morgan to replace John McNamara on July 14, 1988—Bastille Day back in France—they had no idea what they were getting into. The Sox organization had labeled Morgan as the archetypical minor leaguer, a good company man, but not big-league material. He proved them wrong in a stunning and wild ride that came

Manager Joe Morgan shouts instructions from the dugout on Tuesday, October 10, 1990, at the Oakland Coliseum as he watches his team lose a third straight game in the playoffs to the Oakland A's in the American League Championship Series.
(AP Photo/Paul Sakuma)

to be called Morgan's Magic, and wound up with Boston making up the biggest deficit to finish first in franchise history.

It was a remarkably confident Morgan on the afternoon that McNamara was fired. When team president John Harrington approached Morgan about taking over for McNamara until the team could settle on a more experienced skipper, part of the new manager's reply was, "Mr. Harrington, the word 'interim' is not in my vocabulary." Morgan wound up having to wait a day to make his debut behind a major-league bench. The game that night was rained out and rescheduled as part of a doubleheader the next day, with Roger Clemens pitching Game 1.

He was overpowering in a performance that ranked with the best games he ever pitched in a Red Sox uniform. Clemens beat Bret Saberhagen and the Royals 3–1 striking out 16. The Sox won the second game 7–4, and part two of the 1988 season had begun very well. What came to be known as Morgan's Magic started the next afternoon, a warm Saturday at Fenway Park.

Boston played Kansas City in the third game of a four-game series. The Royals had a 6–0 lead after five innings. But the Red Sox got four runs in the last of the sixth and Dwight Evans tied it with a two-run homer in the bottom of the eighth. In the last of the ninth, Kevin Romine led off for Boston. At the time, he was batting .154 and had never, ever hit a home run in 126 major-league at-bats. That changed quickly just two pitches into the inning—Romine lined a home run into the screen to give the Red Sox a 7–6 victory.

On July 19, Mike Smithson took a no-hitter into the seventh and Boston won, 5–0. That made it six in a row, enough for management to remove the "interim" from Morgan's title. He took over as permanent manager on July 20 in a game against the Twins and the Sox celebrated by playing one of the most illogically dramatic, emotional games in franchise history.

Clemens started and had a 5–0 lead through five innings. Minnesota came back and made it 5–4 in the top of the eighth. In the bottom of the eighth, Boston had Ellis Burks on first base with one out and Jim Rice due up. Morgan called Rice back from the on-deck circle and sent up backup shortstop Spike Owen to pinch-hit. Or at least, to pinch-bunt, which is what Owen did successfully. When Rice returned to the dugout, he yelled at the new manager and shoved him, to which Morgan responded, "I'm the skipper of this nine."

Fans around the dugout could hear the commotion and craned their necks to see what was going on, but the altercation was in the runway leading to the clubhouse. Other Sox players broke it up and the game went on, although Rice was later suspended by the team for three games.

Although Owen got the bunt down successfully Burks never scored, and the Twins eventually came back to tie it at 5–5 in the ninth. Minnesota then scored twice in the top of the tenth and it was 7–5. Once again, Morgan's Magic seemed to have reached its end.

While the Twins were rallying, circumstances were evolving that would bring Boston an improbable victory. Over in the third-base grandstand a fan had climbed up one of the support poles for Fenway's ancient roof. He then clambered out onto the guide wire that extended all the way down to the screen behind home plate and supported the screen from the third-base side. Then slowly, deliberately, the fan began to climb down the wire towards the screen, hand over hand, his feet wrapped around the wire, his body hanging over the box seats below.

On the mound was Minnesota reliever Juan Berenguer. Berenguer, a right-hander, had to look directly at the descending fan every time he stopped to set in his motion. By now, Fenway Park was buzzing as some 33,000 or so people watched the trapeze show going on over the visitor's dugout. No one in the ballpark tried to stop the acrobat. The umpires did not stop the game. For his part, Berenguer could not keep his eyes off of the sideshow. He would look at the man on the wire, look at home plate, and throw a pitch—a pitch that was almost always a ball.

Berenguer walked Mike Greenwell, got an out, then walked Owen. Shaken, Berenguer finally walked off the mound and was replaced by Keith Atherton. Jody Reed greeted Atherton with a double off the wall to make it 7–6. Todd Benzinger followed Reed to the plate, worked the count to 2–2, and then hooked a majestic fly ball around Pesky's Pole in right for a game-winning home run; Boston 9, Minnesota 7.

The White Sox came to Fenway for four games and they were swept, too. On July 21, Boyd took a perfect game into the seventh and Boston won, 6–1. On July 24, a Sunday afternoon, Smith came on in the eighth with a one-run lead and struck out four Chicago batters to save a 3–2 victory that concluded an 11–0 homestand.

As the streak continued, Morgan went from having the best start to a Red Sox's managerial career to the best start of any managerial career in baseball history, and the entire nation began to take notice. In a sport where ego and pay stubs had begun to define its most visible figures, Morgan was just the opposite. He would autograph baseballs with the names of dead presidents, toss them into the stands, and watch the reaction as some fan read, "Chester A. Arthur" on his official American League ball. One time, Morgan did that and a little girl about 10-years-old or so got a "Grover Cleveland" ball. She began to cry and Morgan felt so bad that he had her come into the dugout, gave her a ball, and instructed all of the Red Sox players sitting there to sign it.

In Baltimore one time, Morgan discovered that he and *Boston Globe* beat writer Dan Shaughnessy both had gift certificates from the same clothing store for doing local radio appearances. Shaughnessy was headed downtown to cash his in and Morgan figured he would have the writer redeem his certificate as well. Shaughnessy soon found himself bringing $75 worth of boxer shorts back to Morgan's room at the Cross Keys Inn.

The Red Sox are always a national story, and Morgan became a headliner as his record-breaking run as new manager continued. Near the end of that first Fenway homestand, he began to tell reporters about an upcoming interview he had with a TV newsman, Dana Kiecker. We all knew that Dana Kiecker was a pitcher for the Pawtucket Red Sox; when Boston got to Texas for its first road trip under Morgan, he did an interview in the lobby of the Sheraton hotel in Arlington with NBC reporter Douglas Kiker.

The streak continued in Texas on July 25, when Clemens beat the Rangers, 2–0. The night game was played in 100-degree heat and Clemens threw an unimaginable 162 pitches. Boston's 12-game winning streak—its best since 1948—ended on July 26 in a 9–8 loss that left the Sox 2½ games out of first place. A venerable sports adage is that streaks follow streaks, so it seemed reasonable to expect Boston to come back to earth, Morgan's Magic or not, but that was not the case.

The Sox started a new winning streak the next night with a 10–7 victory over the Rangers, which commenced a seven-game winning streak that peaked on August 3 with a 5–4 victory at Fenway, again over the Rangers. With that win, Boston had gone from nine games out of first place to a tie for first in a span of 20 games because 19 of them were victories.

While Morgan was resurrecting the Red Sox's title hopes, general manager Lou Gorman was lining up a major trade. With the Sox having unexpectedly jumped back into contention, Boston became a trade market buyer, not seller. The Sox needed more starting pitching, as they always did; the Orioles had veteran Mike Boddicker to shop around and were looking for prospects to rebuild their team.

Boston was back home on July 29, and had a doubleheader scheduled with the Brewers. It was a Friday, and the menu in the press dining room, where Red Sox executives also ate, included make-your-own sundaes. Gorman, however, was nowhere to be found at lunch time, and he especially loved dessert. There could be only one reason—a trade—and sure enough, the announcement was made later that afternoon. The Sox acquired Boddicker for Brady Anderson, who opened the 1988 season in center field, and minor-league pitcher Curt Schilling.

A typical example of how Morgan thought outside of the average managerial box was in his use of Boddicker one afternoon in 1988. The pitcher was 3–2 in his first five starts for Boston—the fifth was a loss to Seattle on August 18. Boddicker went 5⅓ innings in that game and was next slated to pitch on August 23. On August 20, the Sox played Oakland at Fenway Park. It was a warm Saturday afternoon, the kind of day that pitchers hated for good reason. Both starting pitchers, Todd Burns for the Athletics and Oil Can Boyd for the Sox, were knocked out early and it was a 7–4 score in Boston's favor after just two innings.

The A's then loaded the bases with two out in the sixth. Jose Canseco, representing the go-ahead run, was due up to face Sox reliever Jeff Sellers. Morgan did not like that matchup and brought in Boddicker, who had pitched 5⅓ innings just two days prior, to face Canseco. Boddicker got

Canseco to hit a bouncer right back to the mound and the threat was over. Boston went on to win 7–5 with Boddicker getting three of the 27 outs.

* * *

The Sox began a five-game series in Detroit on August 4 and while the Sox dropped four of five in Tiger Stadium, there was one more trick left in Morgan's Magic.

The Tigers won each of the series' first four games. Boston was back where it had been just eight games into Morgan's Magic and the season was in danger of reverting to form. The Sox lost 4–2 on Saturday, August 6. After the game, reporters filed into a silent Boston clubhouse and entered the manager's office, the smallest one in baseball, a tiny cubicle no bigger than the bathroom in a standard Hampton Inn.

As Morgan began to answer questions, the phone on his little desk rang. No one had ever heard the phone ring before—not Morgan, not even any of the reporters who had covered the team for a long time—and everyone assumed it was a wrong number. It kept ringing, so Morgan eventually picked it up. What ensued was a conversation straight from Bob Newhart.

"Hello.

"Yes, this is he. To whom might I be speaking?

"Dick Duncan, eh. Dick, how are you? What can I do for you?

"I understand, yes…you might be right…that's not a bad idea.

"Dick, you're calling at a bit of an inopportune time. I'm a little busy, but it was nice to hear from you.

"Thanks. You, too. Good-bye."

When he hung up, Morgan was asked who Dick Duncan was.

"Never heard of him before in my life," was the reply. What happened, it turned out, was that a Red Sox fan back home had called the Tiger Stadium switchboard, asked to speak to the manager, and was put through—no questions asked. Morgan handled the call and the ensuing advice with grace despite the fact that his team's season was on the verge of unraveling, then went on to take more questions. The final question had to do with Sunday's game, and Boston's chances at avoiding a sweep with Bruce Hurst on the mound.

"Hurst'll spin a beauty," Morgan said. "We'll win tomorrow and leave here three games out."

The Tigers were horrified by what they perceived as Morgan's arrogance in predicting a victory. But he had managed Hurst in the minors then joined him in the majors when he was promoted to a coaching position. Morgan thought that Hurst was one of the best big-game pitchers he had ever seen, and the lefty's performance in the 1986 postseason bore him out. So, on August 7, 1988, with the Sox in danger of falling five games out of first place, Hurst pitched a sensational 10-inning shutout and Boston won, 3–0.

The Sox eventually made up the three games in the standings they lost in Detroit and the rest of the 1988 AL East title chase became the classic baseball grind. Morgan kept a steady hand, Boddicker turned out to be a life-saving addition to the starting rotation, and Boston eventually won the division title by a game. The Sox were overmatched by the Athletics in the postseason and were swept in the ALCS but that did little to dull the memories left by Boston's improbable run to the title, and the magic that transpired along the way.

CHAPTER 10

ROGER CLEMENS

Some species eat their young—the Red Sox eat their old.

With exception of Bobby Doerr, Ted Williams, and Carl Yastrzemski, Sox superstars leave town like Hansel and Gretel trailing dirty laundry instead of bread crumbs. Dom DiMaggio quit in disgust after being buried on the bench by Lou Boudreau. Luis Tiant left in a huff for New York, Carlton Fisk didn't even receive a contract on time, Mo Vaughn was shown the door with a lowball offer, Dwight Evans was invited to find some other team that might want him, Wade Boggs and Johnny Damon joined the hated Yankees for more money.

And then there was Roger Clemens.

No Red Sox superstar divorce was more bitter than Clemens'. No former Boston player generates more ill will with current Sox fans than does Clemens. When the Sox flirted with the idea of bringing him back at the end of his career, it would have been interesting to see the reaction to him in a Boston uniform again. It was always an uneasy marriage anyway.

Although Clemens was born in Ohio and spent a lot of his youth there, he went to high school in suburban Houston and considered himself a Texan all the way through. While in Boston, he became the emperor of the malaprop, saying things like "I was misinterpretated," or "I've been struggling in all assets of my game." It got to a point where the *Boston Herald* would tape his post-game interviews and print them verbatim in a column called "The World According to Roger."

But the man could pitch. He arrived in the major leagues in 1984, having fast-tracked through the minors where he worked in just 18

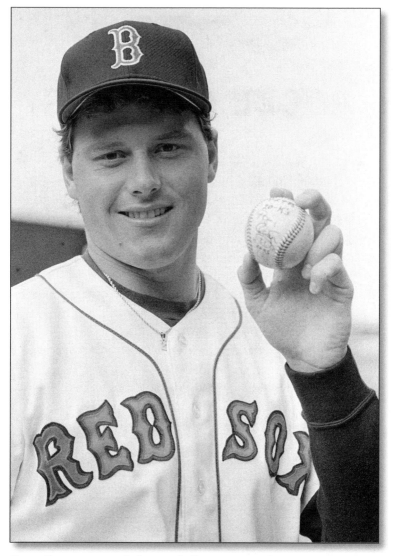

Roger Clemens poses with the game ball at Fenway Park on Wednesday, April 30, 1986. Clemens set an all-time Major League Baseball record by striking out 20 batters in Tuesday night's game against the Seattle Mariners. (AP PHOTO/ELISE AMENDOLA)

games. The Red Sox projected Clemens as someone they could build their franchise around and they were right. After surgery on his right shoulder in 1985, he came back in '86 to go 24–4 and win both the American League Cy Young Award and Most Valuable Player Award.

The problems began right after that, though. Clemens reported to spring training in 1987, but walked out early demanding a bigger contract. He was gone for 29 days and Commissioner Peter Ueberroth finally stepped in to help resolve the holdout. Clemens responded with a second straight Cy Young season.

Through 1992, Clemens put together seven consecutive superb seasons. He won 20 games three times and never won fewer than 17. He never had an ERA higher than 3.13. In 1990, he had his best season, going 21–6 with a remarkable 1.93 earned run average, and '91 and '92 were both good years for him, especially 1992 when he pitched well for the worst Red Sox team since 1966.

In 1993, though, Clemens' performance dropped off dramatically and for the first time since his shoulder surgery in '85, he seemed vulnerable. He spent the middle of the summer on the disabled list with a groin strain, a problem that had bothered him off and on throughout his career because of how much he used his legs in his delivery. His record was below .500 (11–14) for the first time and his ERA climbed higher than 4.00 (4.46) for the first time.

Bad years happen to good players. If Mike Lowell hadn't hit .236 in 2005, the Marlins might never have traded him to the Red Sox. Johnny Damon hit .256 for Oakland in 2001 after hitting .347 in Kansas City the year before, and and he hit .286 in Boston the year after.

Clemens' records in 1994 and 1995 were more like it for him, although his won-lost mark suffered because his team rarely produced many runs for him. In '95, however, Boston won the AL East title and Erik Hanson, not Clemens, was the Sox's best starter. His ERA was more than 4.00 again and for the first time in his major league career—this didn't even happen in 1993—he allowed more hits than innings pitched.

By the end of the 1995 season, the Red Sox had paid Clemens a little more than $30 million for his career. Clemens entered 1996 in the final year of a three-year span in which he was earning about $16 million, and he would be a free agent when the year was over.

Historically, players have their best seasons in their last year before free agency, but Clemens did not. In fact, he had a baffling season in which there were times when he looked like Pat Rapp and times he looked like Cy Young. Clemens went 0–4 before finally winning a game and after a loss to the Royals on August 1, he was 4–11 with a 4.36 ERA. After that August 1 game, in which he allowed 11 hits and seven earned runs in six innings, Clemens skipped his next scheduled start and didn't pitch again until August 11.

The nine days off changed Clemens' season around entirely. He won his next four starts, including a 2–0 shutout of the Angels, and gave up only one run in a span of 33 innings. He came into the season's final games with a chance to catch Cy Young as the Red Sox's all-time winningest pitcher (192), and also to catch up to Young's 38 shutouts in a Boston uniform.

On September 18, Clemens pitched against the Tigers in Detroit one win and one shutout behind Young. On that night, a chilly one in Michigan, Clemens turned the clock back exactly 10 years by striking out 20 in a 4–0 shutout victory. Interestingly, after that game, Clemens was quoted in the *Boston Globe* as saying, "If you work hard enough, good things will happen to you. I know I'm winding down. The wins haven't fallen my way this year."

After Detroit, Clemens could have passed Young in both departments—he had two starts left—but got no run support and went 0–1 in what turned out to be his last two games in a Red Sox uniform. Still, he went 6–2 with a 2.09 ERA in his last 10 starts of 1996, pretty good for a 34-year-old with nearly 2,800 innings pitched in the major leagues.

In the final season of his final year with Boston, Clemens had made $5.5 million. He wanted more, and the Sox were willing to give him more, but he wound up signing with the Blue Jays for $24.75 million over three years. To some extent, fans understand when players opt for more money somewhere else, but Clemens was homegrown and from all accounts Boston made him a legitimate offer. What Clemens wanted, however, along with the money was for the Sox to be almost obsequious in their pursuit of him and they were not.

When the announcement was made that Clemens was headed north, the Red Sox responded with a conference call during which general manager Dan Duquette said something that has been for the most part unfairly reported through the years.

Legend has it that Duquette said that Clemens was "in the twilight of his career," but he did not say that, and what he says comes across much differently in the context of the entire quote, which is:

"The Red Sox and our fans were fortunate to see Roger Clemens play in his prime and we had hoped to keep him in Boston during the twilight of his career. We just want to let the fans know that we worked extremely hard to sign Roger Clemens; we made him a substantial, competitive offer, by far the most money ever offered to a player in the history of the Red Sox franchise.

"Unfortunately, we just couldn't get together. We were hoping he could finish his career as a Red Sox and we also wanted him to establish a relationship beyond his playing career. We wanted him to have the status of a Ted Williams, but at the end of the day we couldn't get it done."

Clemens went up to Toronto and had the best two years of his career in 1997-98. He won consecutive Cy Young Awards and went 41–13 for a team that was 164–160 overall. Much of the hatred Red Sox fans developed for Clemens stems from his first appearance at Fenway Park wearing a uniform other than a Boston one.

That happened on July 12, 1997, and Clemens was as good as he was at his best for the Sox. He pitched eight innings in a 3–1 Toronto victory, striking out 16. In the 1986 game where he struck out 20 Mariners, Clemens had 18 strikeouts after eight innings. Had he managed 18 on July 12, 1997, he might have gone out to the Fenway mound to try for two or three more.

Before the game, as Clemens walked to the bullpen to warm up, his welcome was mixed. There were some cheers and some boos. There were also signs like, "Wanted for treason—William Roger Clemens, alias The Rocket." In the first inning Clemens allowed the first three Boston batters to reach base, one of them Mo Vaughn, who he hit with a pitch, and the Sox jumped ahead, 1–0. After that Clemens was unapproachable, and when he left the mound after the eighth inning, his night's work over, he received a tremendous ovation from the Fenway fans.

He also, it seemed to some, glared into the rooftop box where Duquette sat. Clemens said he did nothing of the sort, that he was looking at family members, and it is like Babe Ruth's called shot, a gesture that can be interpreted any way you wish. While the crowd cheered for Clemens as he departed that night, there was also a sense of wondering why he had not pitched that well for Boston in the final four years of his tenure there.

Clemens pitched twice more versus the Sox in 1997 and had excellent games both times, but did not get any more decisions. Clemens pitched once against the Sox in 1998 and won, but he did not pitch in Boston.

When the Blue Jays signed him—this was not known at the time and the organization was eventually fined because of it—there was an undisclosed clause in his contract that allowed him to ask out if he perceived Toronto was not going to be a contending team. He exercised that after the 1998 season and the Jays traded him to, of all opponents, the Yankees.

Clemens had five great seasons in New York, going 77–36, but he was clearly a different pitcher there than he was in Boston and Toronto, where he chewed up innings. The man who had 18 complete games in 1987 with the Sox had three in five years with the Yankees, and he never once led the American League in strikeouts.

His overall record against Boston was good at 9–5, but that came with a pedestrian ERA of 3.56. He made three postseason starts against the Sox in five years and in those games, all in the ALCS, he was just 1–1 with an 8.18 ERA.

After finishing his career with the Astros and a final season back with the Yankees, Clemens became embroiled in the fallout from the Mitchell Report on steroids. He emphatically denied ever having used them even though his name came up frequently in the report. Even giving Clemens the benefit of the doubt, something had to have happened after he left Boston in 1996 to allow him to rebuild his career.

One possibility is that he had fallen into a rut with the Sox and needed both a change of scene and a symbolic kick in a butt that had gotten substantially larger since his breakthrough season in 1986. Duquette subscribed to that theory and in an interview with Bob Ryan of the *Boston Globe* said, "I think I motivated Roger, don't you? I think I did him a service. One year he came into training camp 45 pounds overweight, another 35. He finally learned the value of keeping yourself in proper condition as you get older."

Another theory is that in Clemens' final years in Boston he got too wrapped up in being the players' spokesman with management and that took away from his on-field performance. Sox ownership in those days was medieval in some ways, and Clemens was constantly battling for things like a player's lounge and better facilities for friends and family who came to the games.

Once he got to Toronto, he was free of those outside concerns and also free of the expectations that went with being a future Hall of Famer in Boston.

Wade Boggs left Boston for the Yankees, and so did Luis Tiant, but Sox fans agreed that Boggs' best days were behind him and they blamed ownership, not Tiant, for his defection. Boston fans likewise blamed Haywood Sullivan, and not Carlton Fisk, for Fisk's move to the White Sox. They also saw the business rationale behind not giving Pedro Martinez what he wanted to stay.

But Clemens was different. Red Sox fans perceived that they had given him their devotion and affection, and he repaid them by getting complacent and lazy in his final years with the team, laughing at them as he kept winning Cy Young Awards in other places.

Forgiveness almost always comes with time for baseball fans, whose very nature is to love players, not hate them. But Clemens' post-Red Sox career seems like the ultimate betrayal, and it may be a very long time before he is treated like family again.

MATT YOUNG'S
NO-HITTER

Three different men with the last name of Young have pitched for the Red Sox; Cy, Matt, and Tim. One is in the Baseball Hall of Fame. Two have pitched no-hitters. Only one has pitched a no-hitter and lost, though, and that was the most unfortunate pitcher in Red Sox history—lefty Matt Young.

Not only did Young pitch a no-hitter and lose it, he pitched a no-hitter that was not recognized by Major League Baseball as a no-hitter.

The game in question was played on the afternoon of April 12, 1992. The Red Sox were a new-look team that year. Just after the 1991 season ended, they fired popular manager Joe Morgan and replaced him with Butch Hobson, who had been part of the 1978 Boston team that lost the Bucky Dent game to the Yankees, and who had moved up the ranks of the Sox farm system as a manager.

Hobson was hired to bring some toughness to the dugout, a quality the Red Sox front office thought was lacking in Morgan despite his two division titles in 3½ seasons.

Young was part of the reason Morgan got fired. General manager Lou Gorman signed Young as a free agent after the 1990 season, but nobody could figure out why. Young's career record at the time was 51–78. He had gone 12–19 for the Mariners in 1985 and was 8–18 for Seattle in 1990—and not only did Gorman sign Young, he gave him $4.5 million for two years.

About the only reason Gorman could have had for signing Young was that he had pitched twice against the Red Sox in 1990 and allowed only one earned run and struck out 12 in 14 innings. There was no denying Young's raw ability; during spring training his teammates hated stepping into the cage against him because he threw bullets and had a great curveball—neither of which usually went where he aimed.

Young's first season in Boston was a disaster, as could have been predicted. He missed half the season with injuries, and when he did pitch he was 3–7 with a 5.18 ERA. The 1991 season turned on a game played at Fenway Park on September 22 against the Yankees. Going into that game, the Red Sox had put themselves into a position to author one of the greatest rebounds in franchise history. Boston was seven games under .500 on August 7, and then won 31 of the next 41 games. On September 22, the Sox had a 5–4 lead over the Yankees with two out in the top of the ninth and a victory would have moved them into first place.

Instead, Jeff Reardon served up a game-tying homer to Roberto Kelly, and Young, on in relief, surrendered two more runs—two walks, a hit batsman, and then Dan Petry gave up a double—and was the loser in a 7–5 game. The Sox never recovered from that defeat and wound up seven games out of first place.

Hobson had Young in his starting rotation to begin the 1992 season and his first outing was the game in Cleveland, coming about 12 hours after Boston had beaten the Indians 7–5 in 19 innings. Young began his '92 season in familiar fashion with a walk, giving a free base to Kenny Lofton to begin the bottom of the first inning, which was almost like giving up a triple, since opposing runners stole on Young like he had duct tape over his eyes. Sure enough, Lofton swiped second and third in succession and stood at third base with one out when Carlos Baerga came up. He hit a ground ball to shortstop that Luis Rivera threw away, and Cleveland had a 1–0 lead.

Charles Nagy was the Indians starter. Boston threatened in the third when catcher John Flaherty, in his first major league at-bat, led off with a double down the third base line. He reached third on a groundout by Wade Boggs but both Jody Reed and Mike Greenwell struck out to end the inning.

In the bottom of the third, Young walked Tribe shortstop Mark Lewis to lead off the inning, then walked Lofton again. Lewis moved up to third on a fielder's choice and with the Boston infield playing back so early in the game, scored on Baerga's ground ball making it 2–0.

Rivera's RBI single got one of those runs back in the top of the fourth and it was a 2–1 game.

Young and Nagy dueled through seven innings, Young gave out walks in the fifth, sixth, and seventh innings. Boston loaded the bases in the sixth but could not score and in the ninth, with reliever Derek Lilliquist on for the Indians, had men at first and second with nobody out but did not score.

The game ended on Mike Greenwell's double-play grounder, and it ended in a sort of stunned silence. The Indians had not gotten a hit, but had won the game. The Red Sox's pitcher had thrown a complete game, had not allowed a hit, but had lost.

There wasn't much reason to celebrate and nobody on the field or in the stands had ever seen anything quite like it.

What most people at the game, fans and players, did not know was that just that past fall, a special rules committee, convened to clean out the increasingly long list of no-hitters, had decided that pitchers who did not allow any hits, but also did not pitch nine innings, were not to be credited with a no-hitter, although they still kept the complete game.

After his game, Young was brought out from the Boston clubhouse and met with reporters in a tiny passageway just outside of the door. He talked about what he had just done, and how it happened, with the resignation of a man who had gotten a 59 on every test he'd ever taken in his life.

"A no-hitter is supposed to be where you strike out the last guy and the catcher goes out and you jump around," Young said. "When you go back to the dugout and hope your team scores another run, it's kind of anti-climactic...it's kind of like being in Purgatory.

"I don't think it's really hit me yet. I'm still so upset about losing that I'm not so upset about losing whatever you want to call it."

And that was the problem—what to call it.

A year earlier, baseball commissioner Fay Vincent had ruled that no-hitters of less than nine innings would no longer be recognized as such, and Sean McAdam of the *Providence Journal* brought that up during the interview.

Finally, Young was asked when he knew that his effort that day was not going to be counted as a no-hitter. He nodded sadly toward McAdam and said, "Not until the Grim Reaper here told me." Later, in talking about his performance Young said, "I would have pitched to them in the bottom of the ninth, but they didn't want to hit. They didn't get any hits and the game's over. People can make all the rules they want."

In the dugout, Sox players treated Young's performance like a no-hitter. They observed the old superstition of not mentioning that the opposition didn't have any hits.

Hobson never considered taking Young, who threw 120 pitches, out of the game. "If I took him out," the manager said, "they'd boo me out of the ballpark, and then when they introduced me (Sunday)." Indians fans did, indeed, let out with a chorus of groans and boos when, during the second game of the doubleheader, a message ran on the scoreboard that said Young's no-hitter would not count.

Boston's best chance to prolong the game and possibly make Young's no-hitter official happened in the ninth when the Sox had men at first and second with nobody out. Jody Reed fouled off a bunt attempt, then hit a long fly ball to deep left-center that should have been enough to get runner Tom Brunansky over to third from second, but Brunansky never tagged up. Greenwell then hit into the double play to end it.

"I feel like scum," said Sox outfielder Phil Plantier. "Our guy pitches a no-hitter and we can't get runs for him to win. I feel like scum."

For the record, the Red Sox recognize Young's performance as a no-hitter and so does the Hall of Fame. How it can be considered a regulation complete game but not a no-hitter is beyond logic, but this is baseball, which at times seems to have been invented to refute logic. After all, a 410-foot shot to right-center in Fenway Park is probably an out, while a 50-foot dribbler down the third base line is liable to be a hit.

As a sidelight to the Young game, his catcher was rookie Flaherty, who made his major-league debut that day. Flaherty is the only man to catch a no-hitter in his first big league appearance.

Later that afternoon, Roger Clemens took the mound for the Red Sox and pitched a two-hit shutout and Boston won 3–0 to split the doubleheader. The Indians wound up with two hits in two games and a split, prompting manager Mike Hargrove to exclaim, "What a country."

Years later, Young was asked about his uniquely memorable performance on that April afternoon in Cleveland and said, "My sister took her kids to Cooperstown, and it's right up there on the wall with the other no-hitters. My nephew thought it was cool that he saw his Uncle Matt in the Hall of Fame. I don't care what the Commissioner's office thinks. The important thing for me is that I'm in Cooperstown on the wall with the rest of the no-hitters."

Flaherty, who wound up having a long career in the majors and becoming a broadcaster, recalled his debut this way, "I knew he hadn't given up any hits, but it didn't feel like you think a no-hitter will feel. You know, the kind of game where the pitcher is in complete control. There was a lot going on in that one."

Young made four more starts after his no-hitter, did not win any of them, and Hobson eventually pulled him from the rotation. For the season, Young wound up with a 0–4 record. His career record with Boston was 3–11. The complete game he pitched on April 12—not a no-hitter, but a complete game—was the last one he ever threw. The Red Sox released Young at the end of spring training in 1993 and he signed with, of all teams, the Indians. That season with Cleveland was his last.

Matt Young—one of only a few pitchers to strike out four batters in a single inning, one of even fewer to pitch a no-hitter and lose. Someday, maybe even the Commissioner's office will wise up and give him official credit for it.

CHAPTER 12

EARL WEBB

Earl Webb's name comes up annually like Punxsutawney Phil, the groundhog with a major in meteorology. Every spring, usually sometime in May or June, some hot hitter threatens the all-time doubles record set by the mysterious Webb with the Red Sox in 1931. Though occasionally approached, Webb's record has never been surpassed.

In 2000, Colorado's Todd Helton had 59 doubles and Toronto's Carlos Delgado had 57. Red Sox shortstop Nomar Garciaparra and Angels outfielder Garrett Anderson both had 56 in 2002 and Lyle Overbay had 53 for the Brewers in 2004, 37 of them by the All-Star break.

Craig Biggio had 56 with the Astros in 1999, but the most tantalizing "just miss" of all was probably by Twins second baseman Chuck Knoblauch, who had 45 doubles when the 1994 season ended prematurely after 109 games. That projected to exactly 67 over a 162-game season.

One of the most fascinating aspects of Webb's record, though, is the man who achieved it. Nowhere else in baseball's endless compendium of lists does his name appear. Webb apparently appeared out of nowhere to hit 67 doubles in 1931, then vanished as quickly as he arrived.

That's not quite true, however.

Webb had an excellent career in the high minors and played in 650 big-league games for five different teams. He spent most of his time as an outfielder but also pitched in the minors. He was a career .306 big-league hitter, a lefty batter who threw right handed, slower than a just-opened bottle of ketchup, and was a poor fielder who led American League outfielders in errors in 1931 with 16.

Although this hit on Monday, September 2, 2002, is only a single, Boston's Nomar Garciaparra belted 57 doubles for the season. He was still 10 shy of Earl Webb's remarkable record of 67 doubles set in 1931.
(AP PHOTO/BETH A. KEISER)

Thus, he was a perfect fit for the downtrodden Red Sox of the early 1930s.

Webb was 32 when Boston traded Bill Barrett to Washington to get him in April 1930. Webb immediately became a regular on a Sox team that lost 102 games and wound up leading Boston in homers with 16, RBIs with 66, and batting average at .323. His 30 doubles, however, were only third best on the team, and there was no hint of what lay ahead for 1931.

He started right away.

Webb averaged a double every two games during that season's first four rainy weeks, a time that featured a lot of rainouts. When Boston began to make up those rainouts with doubleheaders, Webb exploded. In a three-game span that included a twin bill on May 27, he hit six doubles and had 21 after just 34 games.

He hit 18 doubles in July and also lined into a triple play on the 23rd. By the time the Red Sox finished a 29-game homestand on August 5—that's the way the schedule went in those days—Webb had 51 doubles and was hitting .370. By then, newspapers of the time were tracking his assault on the record, which was 64, set by Detroit's George Burns in 1926.

The scrutiny cost Webb.

Actually, those 51 doubles were one less than most of the baseball world had thought Webb had hit. The official scorers of that time didn't have computers, calculators, or video replays, and box scores were filled with errors. On August 4, the American League discovered that as the season progressed, Webb had mistakenly been credited with a double on a hit that was actually a single.

The long homestand was followed by a 17-game road trip, and Webb had begun to feel the pressure. He went 15 games without a double and his average dropped to .350. By the end of August, Webb had 53 doubles in 124 games—still a record pace, but not by much.

The Red Sox returned to Boston in early September for a 23-game homestand, and that proved to be precisely the tonic Webb needed. Doubles began to fly off his bat again, both at Fenway Park and at Braves Field, where the Sox played their Sunday games.

He hit four in four games from September 5–7 and had 59 after 133 games. On September 13 in a 6–5 loss to the White Sox at Braves Field, Webb joined Burns as the only two players in the 60 Club. The next day he went 2-for-4 with a homer in a 12–8 victory over Chicago, then exploded past Burns with an orgy of doubles starting on the 15th.

TED COX

Late in the1974 season, the Red Sox brought up both Jim Rice and Fred Lynn from their Triple A affiliate in Pawtucket, and a year later they helped Boston to the American League pennant, with Lynn being both Rookie of the Year and Most Valuable Player.

For a few days in 1977, it looked like the Sox had done even better with rookie Ted Cox.

Cox was brought up in mid-September of '77 as Boston tried to stay afloat in a tight three-way race in the AL East, a race in which the Yankees eventually nosed out both the Sox and Orioles by two games. Cox was inserted into the starting lineup for a game in Baltimore on September 18, batting second as the designated hitter in front of a crowd of 51,798. He began his major-league career with a first-inning single to left field. He then reached base in each of his next six times up, five of those plate appearances resulting in hits. Cox's 6-for-6 start set a major-league record that had not been broken as of 2008.

Here's the running tally on Cox's record streak.

On the 18th, he singled in the first, walked in the third, singled in the fifth, singled in the sixth, and doubled in the ninth as Boston won, 10–4. The next day, versus the Yankees back at Fenway Park, with Cox again the DH and again hitting in the No. 2 spot, he lined a single between first and second in the first inning, then singled to right-center in the third.

That made him 6-for-6. In the fifth, somebody finally got Cox out. He grounded to New York first baseman Chris Chambliss and the streak was over.

Years later, Cox recalled his streak in an interview for *Baseball Almanac* with Darl DeVault, remembering that when he came up after his fifth hit, the crowd was, "going nuts. They gave me a standing ovation. You know how they put your photo and stats up on the scoreboard—well, for me it was awesome. I looked up there and my average was 1.000 with five at-bats. I looked back at the Yankees catcher, Thurman Munson, and asked him what I should do. He told me, 'I dunno, tip your hat to 'em. Just shut these people up.'"

Even after Yankees starter Ed Figueroa finally got Cox out in the fifth, the fans kept cheering. "The streak was over and I'm heading back to the dugout when the crowd gave me another standing ovation," he said. "The regulars told me to acknowledge that standing O as well, so I came back out of the dugout and tipped my hat a second time. Reporters later told me mine was the best start ever in the history of the game."

Alas, Cox was neither Rice nor Lynn. After the 6-for-6 start, he finished 21-for-58 in 17 games. In the spring of 1978, Cox was traded to Cleveland as part of the Dennis Eckersley trade, which turned out to be a great deal for the Red Sox. Cox played with four different teams, was never a regular in the majors, and after the perfect beginning he hit .239 the rest of the way.

Cox's last big-league experience was with Toronto in 1981. After his baseball career ended, Cox played professional Slo-Pitch softball, coached youth teams in his native Oklahoma, and worked with the Major League Baseball Players Alumni Association raising money for charity.

Even Lou Gehrig's "unbreakable" record fell. Perhaps Cox's will last even longer.

Webb went 11-for-21 with six doubles in a span of five games. The record toppled in a doubleheader against the Indians at Fenway on September 17. He tied it with a double to left in the first inning of the first game then he hit No. 65 in an almost identical spot in the ninth inning of the second game.

The next day, Burns sent him a congratulatory telegram. Webb doubled again in the first game of a doubleheader on the 18th and was expected to get to 70, but went into a slump. His 67th and final double came on the last day of the season in Washington.

It had taken Webb five years to pass Burns and the press predicted that the new record would last at least five years—and maybe longer. Several players took a shot at it in those five years with the Cardinals' Joe Medwick coming closest with 64 in 1936. No one has hit as many as 60 since '36, however.

Seventy-five years after the doubles record was set, Webb remains a fascinating subject because of the way he appeared virtually out of nowhere then disappeared. He never hit more than 30 doubles in any other major league season and does not hold any other records.

Webb obviously hit some sort of wave just right in 1931. He was healthy, playing in all but two of Boston's 153 games, and hit cleanup all year long, so he had plenty of at-bats. The Fenway Park of his day was a radically different ballpark from today's, with a lower left-field wall that was about 10 feet further from home plate and featured an embankment; an angled corner in right; and wide-open spaces in right-center, with dead-center more than 500 feet away from home plate. Webb was a left-handed hitter with the ability to go the other way, so he used the wall and embankment in left to his advantage, much like Fred Lynn and Wade Boggs did with the Green Monster many years later.

Webb also played in what turned out to be the Golden Age of doubles. Only six players have had as many as 60 doubles in a season, and all of those came in a 10-year span from 1926 to 1936.

Legend has it that as the record got closer Webb would sometimes stop at second on balls that looked like triples. The day after he broke the record, a story in the *Boston Globe* mentioned it, but added that every player who had set or approached the doubles record in the past was accused of doing that.

Not once in any game reports from the 1931 season is it ever mentioned that Webb dogged it on a double. And at the time, Webb had no way of knowing that his record would hold up for as long as it has, just as nobody knew in 1941 that Ted Williams would be the last .400 hitter for decades.

Less than a year after he set the doubles record, Webb was traded to the Tigers for Dale Alexander and Roy Johnson, two players just like him—fine hitters with no speed and little defensive skill. Alexander went on to win the American League batting title that year. When the trade was made on June 13, 1932, Webb had hit just nine doubles in 52 games.

His big-league career was over at the end of the 1933 season, but after that he went back to the minors and played for four more seasons. In 1934, with the Milwaukee Brewers, Webb led the Double A American Association (the equivalent of today's Triple A) in hitting with a .368 average.

After retiring in the summer of 1937, Webb lived in Kopperston, West Virginia, where he worked as a coal miner and coached the local baseball team. He died on May 23, 1965, after a pleasant day of fishing in the mountains. In 2002, some 37 years after Webb's death, the West Virginia Legislature passed a resolution honoring him. It said, in part:

"In addition to the enduring accomplishment of hitting the most doubles in a major league season, he was also a man known by his family and others for his size, strength, and expertise in training bird dogs; deadliness of his aim with guns, the violence of his response to an insult, and the warmth of his compassion for children."

When Webb died, 34 years had passed since he set the record for most doubles in a season. In the years since his death, Lou Gehrig's ironman record was surpassed and first Babe Ruth's then Roger Maris' home run record fell—but nobody has caught Earl Webb.

CHAPTER 13

DR. STRANGEGLOVE

Aside from the 1920s, which the Red Sox spent in or near last place in the American League, the franchise's darkest days came during the pre- and post-Williams years in the 1960s, after the retirement of Ted and before the hiring of Dick. Boston had some pretty good players—Frank Malzone, Eddie Bressoud, Carl Yastrzemski, Bill Monbouquette, Dick Radatz—but many more Bob Heffners, Bob Tillmans, and Felix Mantillas. The most memorable of all of the many one-dimensional Sox of the Sixties, though, was Dick Stuart.

Stuart could hit for power, but do little else, but that didn't seem to matter. There was little to cheer about other than Stuart and Dick Radatz during the 1963 and '64 seasons, and Stuart was so popular he even had his own little studio talk show on Channel 4.

His fielding was so bad that in his second season with the Sox, Stuart became known as "Dr. Strangeglove," a takeoff on the anti-war movie *Dr. Strangelove* that was released in January 1964. In two seasons with the Red Sox, Stuart was charged with 53 errors, 29 in 1963 and 24 in 1964. Those totals led the team in both years—Stuart made more errors than either his third basemen or shortstops—and led the American League in errors by first basemen.

No other first baseman reached even 20 in a season. Joe Pepitone of the Yankees came closest with 18 in 1964. Where Kevin Youkilis once had a 238-game errorless streak at first for the Sox, Stuart's longest errorless streak was 26 games, the first 26 he played in a Boston uniform. After that, he never went longer than 16 straight games without committing an error.

Dick Stuart (7), infielder for the Boston Red Sox, is shown in March 1963.
(AP PHOTO)

When he was with the Pirates, before arriving in Boston, Stuart's manager was Danny Murtaugh who supposedly, after hearing the standard pregame announcement, "Anyone who interferes with a ball in play will be removed from the ballpark," said, "I hope Stuart doesn't think it means him."

Comparing error totals era to era is tough, but it is a reasonable guess that Stuart was the worst every-day defensive player in Red Sox history.

One thing was certain—things happened with Stuart around, not all of them good, but on the night of August 19, 1963, the future Dr. Strangeglove turned into Dr. Strangebat when he did something nobody before him had done, and nobody after him has accomplished. He hit an inside-the-park home run to straightaway left field off the Green Monster.

Most Fenway Park inside-the-park home runs fall into two categories—they go down the right-field line and make a big loop toward the bullpens as they bounce around the curve of the grandstand, or they wind up in no-man's land near the triangle in right-center.

The Red Sox team that played Cleveland on the night of August 19, 1963, was fading fast. The club had started the year with a lot of promise. It had responded well to new manager Johnny Pesky and Stuart had done his part by providing, as advertised, a ton of offensive production. The '63 Sox were relatively close to the American League lead into July and on July 21 were tied for third place, just 7½ games behind the Yankees.

Boston won just 8-of-28 games after that, though, and was just counting down the days until the season ended when it played Cleveland that night.

The opposing starters were lefty Arnold Earley for Boston and Pedro Ramos for the Indians. Ramos retired the Sox in order in the first and it was a 0–0 game when Stuart, batting cleanup, led off the bottom of the second with a lazy fly ball to left-center.

The Indians' center fielder was Vic Davalillo, who stood only 5'7". The left fielder was John Romano, a catcher playing the outfield for the second time in his five-year major league career; the first time was just the day before.

The hardest play for an outfielder to make in Fenway, and it is especially hard for a visiting outfielder, is the in-between fly ball—a fly ball that isn't hit far enough to definitely be off or over the wall, but is hit far enough so it might be off the wall. Like this one by Stuart.

Davalillo decided he could make the catch, but the ball barely scraped the wall on its way down and deflected off Davalillo's forehead, rolling some 100 feet into the left-field corner. The race was on.

Romano, running like a catcher, went to retrieve the ball. Stuart, running like a man with one career stolen base in 676 games, took off around the bases. By the time Romano got to the ball, Stuart was just about out of energy as he went around third base.

The relay throw and Stuart arrived at home plate almost simultaneously, but Stuart slid under the tag and was safe.

"That's the fastest I've run in a long time," Stuart told reporters after the game. "I saw the ball ricochet over towards left field. After that, I just started running. I started to run out of steam after I reached third, took too wide a turn and stumbled.

"Pretty good for a guy who hasn't stolen a base in five years. Of course, they never give me the steal sign."

Davalillo stayed in the game even though he had a lump the size of small egg just over his right eye from where the ball hit him.

"I could have jumped for the ball, too, but let Vic try for it because he's the more experienced outfielder," said Romano.

Stuart hit another home run in the game, sending a shot over the screen in left to lead off the ninth, so his homers provided the first and last Red Sox runs in the game. In between, the Indians hit three home runs of their own, scored eight times, and won, 8–3.

Stuart wound up with 42 home runs for the season, second to Minnesota's Harmon Killebrew. Stuart led the league in RBIs, however, with 118 while teammate Carl Yastrzemski won the batting title with a .321 average. Although their players won two-thirds of the American League Triple Crown, the Red Sox finished in seventh place, 28 games behind the Yankees.

As of 2008, only seven Boston players have had conventional homers and inside-the-park homers in the same game. Stuart was the fourth to do it and the first in 24 years.

Unlike hockey, baseball does not have a plus-minus way to rate players, but Bill James has devised some statistical tools that do something similar. Stuart ranks as the worst "percentage player" to ever play the game. But Stuart did have a knack for creating and witnessing baseball history. He was on deck when Bill Mazeroski homered to win Game 7 of the 1960 World Series, and in 1969, Stuart was the first player to return to the major leagues after having left to play in Japan.

In a perverse and indirect way, Stuart probably had something to do with the success that would finally come the Red Sox's way in 1967. One of Stuart's teammates on the '63 and '64 team was Dick Williams, who once said that Stuart was the most selfish player he had ever seen, and who watched from a distance as Pesky was taunted and ignored by Stuart while an unsupportive general manager, Mike Higgins, stood idly by.

Something like that would never happen were Williams ever to become a manager, and he did in 1967, at which time Stuart was playing in Japan and the memories of his inside-the-park home run had become part of Red Sox legend.

CHAPTER 14

THE GREATEST MANAGER

Just before Joe Morgan left for a road trip to Texas, and just before his team was about to take the field at Fenway Park and win its 11th game in a row, he sat in his office with a group of reporters, reflected on the amazing streak the Red Sox had put together after his Bastille Day hiring, and opened his mail.

Out from a white envelope dropped a succinct piece of advice from a would-be manager. The note read, "Joe, you're using the wrong lineup."

The ultimate fate of any manager, but particularly a Red Sox manager, is to be blamed for things that are not really his fault and to be cast in some light that makes him seem like a blundering idiot. It goes with the territory, but the pay is good and the potential rewards inviting, so somebody always applies for the job when it opens up.

One applicant in particular who succeeded beyond anyone's hopes, or at least beyond what anyone dared hope, was Terry Francona, who was picked to replace Grady Little after the unhappy carnage of the 2003 ALCS.

Francona had spent four miserable years managing bad Phillies teams from 1997 to 2000, then got released, and has said, looking back on those years, "I should have been fired." He spent a year in the Indians baseball operations department, a year as Rangers bench coach, and a year as Oakland's bench coach before applying for the vacant Boston job.

With Francona in charge, the Red Sox won a World Series in his first year as manager, then won another three seasons later. Not bad for someone whose nickname had been "Francoma." Not bad for someone who took over a team that had not won a World Series in 86 years.

Terry Francona—the best manager in Red Sox history?

Maybe so, but there are a lot of managers and a lot of history to sort through before that claim can be substantiated, a history that goes all the way back to the founding of the franchise, when Hall of Famer Jimmy Collins was a player-manager and won two pennants and one World Series in 5½ years.

Collins was considered to be so good at what he did that the Sox paid him $12,000 a year—awfully good money for those days and more than the major league minimum salary for about the next 70 years.

Was Collins the best Boston manager ever? Nah, and it's not Francona, either. Here is a subjective ranking of the best and worst Red Sox managers through the years.

1. Dick Williams, 1967–69

Francona took a good team that was one game away from being in the World Series in 2003 to being a champion. Williams took a ninth place team, a half-game from last place, and a moribund franchise, and won a pennant in the greatest race in American League history, thus creating a foundation for someone like Francona to build on.

The 1966 Red Sox were 72–90, and the 1967 Red Sox went 92–70. Attendance in '66 was 811,172. Attendance in '67 was 1,727,832. It wasn't all due to Williams, but a lot of it was. He drove his players to excel and they often hated him for it, but the "country club" atmosphere that had prevailed in the Boston organization throughout the years of Yawkey ownership disappeared under Williams.

After 1967, Willliams' Sox finished 17 games out, then 22 games out. He was actually fired just before the end of the 1969 season, and it turned out to be a mistake. Boston's record in '69 was 87–75. In 1970, under his replacement, Eddie Kasko, it was 87–75—exactly the same.

This is Hall of Famer Dick Williams in 2006. Never before in Red Sox history has a manager done so much for the team in so short a tenure.
(AP Photo/Steven Senne)

In '71, Boston was 85–77, not even as good as Williams' last year in charge.

Williams won World Series championships with Oakland in both 1972 and 1973, and won the first pennant in franchise history with the San Diego Padres in 1984. He is in the Baseball Hall of Fame, and as a career .260 hitter, Williams' selection was not as a player.

He was one of the best managers in baseball history, so why should it be a surprise that Dick Williams is the best manager, period, in Red Sox history?

2. Terry Francona, 2004–

In a market like Boston, there is a temptation for managers to do some things just so people will shut up. One of Francona's strengths is his absolute refusal to do that. One time, while talking about what he learned from his four horrible seasons managing the Phillies, he said after that experience he understood how important it was to follow his own instincts and not worry about what anybody else thought was the right thing to do.

That sort of quiet self-confidence first showed up in the 2004 playoffs. After Boston had swept the Angels in the Division Series, they played the Yankees in the ALCS. The Red Sox lost the first three games of that series and in doing so, the very top of the Boston batting order—Johnny Damon and Mark Bellhorn—combined to be just 2-for-25. Francona refused to bench either of them, although he did drop Bellhorn down in the batting order, and both players responded by being key offensive contributors in the Red Sox's comeback to take the series in seven games and eventually go on to capture the World Series.

In 2007, which ended once again in a Red Sox World Championship, Francona's team built a huge mid-season lead in the AL East race, a lead that on July 5 had stretched to 11½ games over the Yankees. In September, New York got hot, Boston got hurt, and the Yankees began to close the gap.

Even though a Wild Card playoff berth was ensured, fans howled for the Sox to do something to hold off the Yanks—the Ghosts of '49, '78 and '03 die hard—but Francona rested his key players, set up his pitching staff for the postseason, was able to keep his team in first place anyway, and took it all the way again.

Sometimes, doing nothing is the way to win. Francona figured that out in Philadelphia and took it with him to Boston.

In some ways, Francona does not seem like a good fit for the Boston market. He is from a baseball family, and save for about a day as a prospective real estate agent—"I wasn't gonna sell any houses, anyway" he said when he quit to become a coach—has not had a career outside of baseball. Francona has simple tastes—his favorite restaurant is the Cracker Barrel, he hates driving in rotaries, and is usually behind the wheel of the slowest car on the road.

Red Sox fans reserve the right to question his strategic moves, but most of them work out. Francona keeps his regular position players healthy by resting them on occasion which also keeps his bench guys sharp, and uses his bullpen judiciously. What drives fans crazy, though, is how he never, ever criticizes a player no matter how obvious a mistake might have been, or how atrocious an action was.

Francona's view is that part of his job description is making it easier for his players to perform, and one way to do that is to deflect criticism. It can be a maddening trait at times, but it helped him win two World Series in four years.

3. Bill Carrigan, 1913–16; 1927–29

Carrigan's career record managing the Red Sox was 489–500—he finished in the red. That's because his second stint with the team happened during the franchise's darkest days, when the talent in Boston was barely as good—and maybe not even as good—as some of the best teams in the high minors.

"Bill was a good manager," remembered Milt Gaston, the centenarian who pitched for Carrigan the second time around, "but he just didn't have a pitching staff."

The contrast in Carrigan's records is stark. He was 323–205 in his first tour of duty with the Red Sox, when he was a player-manager, and 166–295 in the late 1920s. The most important numbers in Carrigan's resume are his two World Series championships. He and Francona are the only two Boston managers to win more than one World Series.

Carrigan was a native of Maine and played college baseball at Holy Cross, but had a reputation for physical toughness. That surely helped in how he was able to handle Babe Ruth, who played his first three major league seasons under Carrigan's management.

4. Joe Morgan, 1988–91

The Red Sox had never considered Morgan as anything more than a good soldier and when they fired John McNamara on July 14, 1988, Sox ownership wanted Morgan to run the team for a few days until they found a real manager, maybe someone like Joe Torre.

Instead, Boston won its first 12 games in a row with Morgan in charge and went 19–1 in the first 20. The Sox went on to win the AL East title and, until Morgan was fired after the end of the 1991 season, they won two divisional titles, finished second, and finished third.

He was immensely popular with fans, and had a good won-lost record, so why did Morgan get fired? There was never a good explanation, and owner Jean Yawkey died not long after the firing, but the most likely reason is that Sox players didn't like the fact that Morgan refused to lie for them and try to cover for them when they fouled up. It also could have been that Mrs. Yawkey took a liking to Pawtucket Red Sox manager Butch Hobson, a charming southern gentleman, and let her feelings dictate who should run the team.

In evaluating Morgan, a couple of things are worth noting: His predecessor, John McNamara, went 121–126 in the 1½ seasons before Morgan took over. Hobson, his successor, went 207–232 in about 2½ seasons. With Morgan managing in the middle of those two, the Red Sox went 301–262.

5. Jimmy Collins, 1901–06

Collins was a player-manager and the best third baseman of his time. The way his managerial career ended colors the way his overall performance is viewed. During the 1906 season, to date the second worst in franchise history, Collins simply stopped showing up for work. There were reasons for that—his relationship with owner John I. Taylor had soured—but people are still expected to show up for work even if their boss is a jerk. However, Collins was a huge reason Boston's team in the new American League immediately overtook the National League franchise as the No. 1 team in town.

Collins' Boston Americans finished four games out of first in 1901, 6½ out in 1902, won the pennant and World Series in 1903, and won the pennant in 1904 when the New York Giants refused to play the World Series. After the 1904 season, during which Collins employed five pitchers for the entire year—Bill Dinneen made 37 starts and had 37 complete games—the Americans got cold almost overnight and Collins was officially gone as manager at the end of August in 1906.

6. Jake Stahl, 1912–13

Perhaps Stahl looks as good as he does because he never had enough time to fail, but his one full season as Red Sox manager resulted in the best full season a Boston team has ever had. Stahl replaced Patsy Donovan when the team moved from the Huntington Avenue Grounds to Fenway Park in 1912. The Sox went 105–47 for their best regular season ever, then beat the New York Giants, four games to three, in one of the most dramatic World Series ever played.

The 1913 Red Sox, like the 1976 and '96 teams decades later, followed up a first-place finish with a complete flop. The 1913 Sox were two games under .500 when Stahl was fired by owner James McAleer on July 15, who had heard unsubstantiated rumors that Stahl wanted to replace him as team president. Stahl's successor was catcher Bill Carrigan, and Carrigan at least got the club over .500.

Even with the 1913 record bringing his overall mark down, Stahl finishing 144–88 is the best won-lost record for any full-time Red Sox manager ever.

7. Fred Lake, 1908–09

Lake is one of the most interesting but obscure figures in early Red Sox history. He was working as a scout for Boston in 1908 when Deacon McGuire was fired as manager. Lake took over a team that was 53–62 and went 22–17 the rest of the way. Then, in 1909, he managed the Sox up into third place and finished just 9½ games out of first. This was a team that went 108–195 in 1906 and 1907. On August 24, 1909, Lake had the Red Sox, a team that since 1904 had not been able to see first place with binoculars, just 1½ games out of the league lead. At the end of the 1909 season, Lake asked for a raise and didn't get it. In fact, he was fired instead.

Lake's Sox had finished 9½ games out of first place in 1909. Under Patsy Donovan, Boston was 22½ games out in 1910 and 24 games out in 1911.

8. Ralph Houk, 1981–84

Houk is one of the handful of Red Sox managers who left on his own. He was a surprise choice to replace Don Zimmer after the failed Boston dynasty of the late 1970s fell apart. Houk was 61 when he took the job and during his four years as manager, he kept a franchise with very mediocre talent respectable mostly with his adept handling of the pitching staff.

Houk's first season, 1981, was a strike year and played in two halves. Houk had Boston in contention for the second-half AL East title until the final few days of the season. In 1982, with a mediocre roster, Houk had the Red Sox in first place into early July and had the team still in contention on Labor Day before it faded.

By the end of the 1984 season, Houk was nearing 65 and he retired, but not before he watched Roger Clemens pitch his first game in the major leagues.

9. Joe McCarthy, 1948–50

Just think—McCarthy was two games away from probably being considered the greatest Red Sox manager of all time. If his Red Sox had won the playoff game against the Indians in 1948 or one of the two final games of the 1949 season in Yankee Stadium, he would be one of just three Boston managers to have won back-to-back pennants, along with Collins and Carrigan, both ranked above him. As it is, McCarthy is one of just three Sox full-time skippers with a career winning percentage in the .600s.

For the Boston teams of the late 1940s, McCarthy was a good fit. They were veteran teams and he left most of his players, particularly Ted Williams, alone. McCarthy was very much like Terry Francona in that he never was critical of a player in public. Red Sox fans, though, never really forgave McCarthy for two things—he had managed some great Yankees teams that beat very good Boston teams, and he could never win the last game of the season.

10. Jimy Williams, 1997–2001

There is only one word that truly encompasses the puzzle that was Jimy Williams and that is "inscrutable." Williams' tortured syntax was almost impossible to decipher, which is how he wanted it, and when questioned about strategic moves he more often than not responded with "manager's decision" and just let everyone wonder.

Williams had been a player, coach, or manager for more than 35 years when he was hired by Dan Duquette for the 1997 season, and while the Sox have had other managers who knew as much baseball as Williams, they have never had one who knew more.

Here's an example of how things worked with Williams. In the sixth inning of game in Montreal on July 15, 2001, the Red Sox had Hideo Nomo on the mound and a 6–3 lead, but the Expos were rallying with runners on first and second, nobody out, and Mark Smith up. Nomo got to a point where he had two strikes on Smith then Williams lifted him in favor of Garces, who finished the at-bat with a walk.

Boston eventually won the game 8–5, and I asked Williams afterward why he waited until there were two strikes on Smith before making the move to Garces. "Manager's decision" was the curt reply, and I walked out of the little press meeting in disgust.

The next day, Williams pulled me aside and explained that it was a bunt situation, and he did not want Garces—who weighed around 300 pounds—fielding any bunts. So he waited until two strikes, when the bunt was no longer an option. It was a perfectly valid reason, but why the secrecy?

Williams got Boston into the playoffs in 1998 and 1999, with the '99 team winning a postseason series for the first time since 1986. He had the Red Sox in contention into August in 2001, but when the team slumped Duquette fired him and replaced him with pitching coach Joe

Kerrigan. Boston was 65–53 when Williams was canned; it was 17–26 for Kerrigan, who didn't make it to 2002.

That's a subjective list of the Red Sox's best managers; what about the worst? There are plenty of candidates and here are the bottom five.

1. Mike Higgins, 1955–59; 1960–62

Higgins has come to personify all that was wrong with the Red Sox from the time they stopped being contenders in the late 1940s to the Impossible Dream season. And why not? None of Higgins' teams ever remotely contended for a pennant, and he was at the forefront of the racists who kept the franchise lily white and in the second division until Pumpsie Green made his debut in 1959.

Midway through the 1959 season, with the Red Sox 11 games under .500 and in last place, Higgins was finally fired and replaced by Billy Jurges. Jurges provided an instant shot of adrenaline, then the Sox became the Sox and midway through the 1960 season he was fired and replaced by Higgins of all people. It was one thing to hire him in the first place, but to bring him back? After 2½ more years under .500, Higgins was finally promoted to general manager, and if anyone wonders why the Red Sox were so bad for so long all they have to do is look at Mike Higgins' career in the organization for the answer.

2. Joe Kerrigan, 2001

Jimy Williams was fired on the afternoon of August 16, 2001, and the Red Sox scheduled a press conference to announce his successor in a modest meeting room under the left-field grandstand. Things had happened quickly—there was no hint as to who Williams' successor might be, or whether the team was just going to hire someone to get it through the end of the season, or go after a long-term manager.

One possibility was Gene Lamont, Williams' third base coach, who had managed parts of eight seasons with the White Sox and Pirates. If there was a most likely candidate, it was Lamont. Instead, general manager Dan Duquette stunned the reporters in the meeting room when he strode through the door accompanied by, in uniform, pitching coach Joe Kerrigan.

Make that former pitching coach Joe Kerrigan, who had just signed a contract to manage the Sox for the rest of the 2001 season and for two more years after that—even though he had never managed a game before in his life.

Kerrigan's lack of experience showed immediately. In the sixth inning of his first game as manager, an eventual 6–4 victory by Boston, Kerrigan stayed in the dugout as first baseman Jose Offerman argued a called third strike with plate umpire Wally Bell, arguing long enough to warrant an ejection. Kerrigan had been an excellent pitching coach, but had no real knowledge of the offensive side of the game, how to run a game, or even how to put together a lineup and batting order.

When Williams was fired, Boston had lost six of seven games but was in second place in the AL East, 12 games above .500, and just five games out of first. Considering the problems Williams had with his lunatic center fielder, Carl Everett, things were not so bad. As it turned out, Williams was not the problem—he was the solution.

After getting off to a decent beginning under Kerrigan—Boston went 6–3 in his first nine games and closed to within three games of first—the team lost an 8–7 game in 18 innings at Texas with Kerrigan making several strategic mistakes. That set the Red Sox off on a nine-game losing streak and a skid that eventually turned into 1–13. By the end of it, Boston was 13 games out of first and out of Wild Card contention, too.

When ownership officially changed during spring training of 2002, Kerrigan was out of a job, but not out of money, at least for two more years.

3. Lou Boudreau, 1952–54

If the Red Sox had hired Boudreau as their manager in 1947, they might have won the pennant in 1948, since he would not have been the shortstop-manager who led the Indians to an 8–3 victory in the pennant playoff at Fenway Park.

When they did hire him, he went about destroying the remnants of the excellent postwar Sox teams and started the franchise down a road that led to 15 years of misery.

Boudreau actually joined the Sox in 1951 after the Indians had fired him as player-manager. He spent the '51 season as a utility infielder under Steve O'Neill, and when O'Neill had health problems he took over as manager for the 1952 season. Boudreau actually played in four games in '52 and remains Boston's last player-manager.

The Boudreau years saw the Red Sox try to rebuild the aging core of the team that almost won the pennant in 1948 and '49. Bobby Doerr retired. Dom DiMaggio did, too, after Boudreau reduced him to a bench player. Johnny Pesky was traded. In '52, the Sox finished under .500 for the first time in seven years. They bounced back above .500 in '53, but finished 69–85 and 42 games out of first place the next year, their worst season since the war year of 1943.

Boudreau was fired and replaced by Higgins. Little did Sox fans know things were going from bad to worse.

4. Billy Jurges, 1959–60

The hiring of Jurges to replace Higgins during the 1959 season was as surprising at the time as the decision to hire Kerrigan in 2001. Jurges had no previous managerial experience and was the third-base coach of the Washington Senators when the Sox called. Jurges continued coaching third as Red Sox manager, and he is the last Boston manager to act as his own third-base coach.

Boston's general manager at the time was Bucky Harris, who had spent much of his career in the Senators organization and was friends with Jurges. The move worked at least as well, in the short term. The Red Sox were in last place when Jurges was hired and went 44–36 the rest of the way and finished fifth.

Jurges, however, did not have a very good temperament for the job of major league manager, especially in a city like Boston. He was high strung and jittery and it all came crashing down one year later when, after the team got off to a dismal start, Jurges was quoted by Clif Keane of the *Boston Globe* as saying, "I know what's wrong with this club but I can't do anything about it. My hands are tied."

Jurges left to go home on June 8 for a rest and never came back. Higgins, however, did.

5. George Huff, 1907

A look at the official listing of managers in the Red Sox media guide shows Huff going 2–6 in 1906, a season during which the team employed four different managers. Eight games as manager? Surely Huff was an interim skipper until Boston could sort things out, but he wasn't. Huff was hired full-time and quit after less than two weeks on the job.

Huff replaced Cy Young, who had replaced Chick Stahl, who had killed himself during spring. Before being named manager in Boston, Huff was Athletic Director at the University of Illinois and a scout for the Cubs. The veteran players thought his hiring was a joke and lost six of eight under him before Huff got the message and went back to Illinois.

He stayed in the organization as a scout, and in that role he contributed to the franchise's upcoming glory days by signing outfielder Tris Speaker near the end of the season.

Those are the worst five. What about Don Zimmer? What about Grady Little? Neither were terrible managers. Both just failed at the wrong time, Zimmer during the collapse of 1978 and Little in Game 7 of the 2003 ALCS. It can be said of Little that the 2004 Red Sox really got their start under him in 2003. Francona came along, took what they had learned under Little, and made the right moves in the postseason, which is why Francona is near the top of the Sox's all-time best managers list and Little is not even on it.

KEVIN KENNEDY

One of Kevin Kennedy's favorite sayings when he was managing the Red Sox was that baseball is a results business, and there is little room for sentiment or subjectivity in making decisions. Kennedy got results in his two years managing in Boston, but was fired anyway.

He was hired by general manager Dan Duquette after the 1994 season, the third straight under manager Butch Hobson, and the third straight in which the Red Sox failed to win more than they lost. Kennedy and Duquette knew each other from the Expos organization, and Kennedy had previously managed in the major leagues with the Rangers.

In 1995, Kennedy took a team that had gone 54–61 the year before—a season ended prematurely by a labor dispute—and took it to the AL East title. The

Red Sox manager Kevin Kennedy looks on as his team loses to the Cleveland Indians 7–6 on Sunday, April 14, 1996, at Fenway Park. The Sox were 2–9 on the season—one of their worst starts in 70 years. (AP Photo/Susan Walsh)

'95 team led the division essentially wire to wire and finished seven games ahead, then suffered a disappointing loss to the Indians in the first round of the playoffs.

In 1996, Kennedy's Sox had an unbelievably bad start, especially for a defending divisional champion. Eighteen games into the season they were just 3–15 and never once touched first place. Kennedy blamed traveling secretary Steve August for putting together a lousy spring training schedule, the Sox fired coaches—even bullpen coach Dave Carlucci—and Duquette made some personnel moves.

The season was rescued and while Boston never contended, it finished with a respectable 85–77 record as Kennedy held things together.

Kennedy was unquestionably full of himself. He had pictures of Hollywood actresses, particularly Natalie Wood, on the walls of the Fenway Park office. He once told a group of bewildered reporters that he took six showers a day and people who took a lot of showers were always successful. He said doctors had told him he was in the top two percent when it came to healing from injuries.

Kennedy made no apologies for the way he treated his players. His philosophy was that superstars like Jose Canseco and Roger Clemens were dealt with differently than the fringe guys, and if a rookie made a mistake, Kennedy would issue a warning shot by telling the media that the major leagues were "not player development."

Kennedy did not think he was being paid enough and went public with his dissatisfaction with the team's contract extension offer after the 1995 season. He told the *New York Times*, "Quite frankly, I'm hurt. What they offered would be a normal raise for any manager. What's the reward for winning?"

That was the beginning of the end. Kennedy found out what the reward was for not winning when he was released after the end of the 1996 season. He never managed again, but stayed in baseball as a television analyst and made occasional return trips to Fenway Park.

CHAPTER 15

JOHNNY DAMON

The winter between the 2005 and 2006 baseball summers was about as bleak and depressing as it gets for Red Sox fans, rivaled perhaps only by the winter of 1919-20, when Babe Ruth was sold to the Yankees.

In the wake of a disappointing loss to the White Sox in the Division Series, general manager Theo Epstein quit—sort of—and that caused some consternation and general gnashing of teeth, but Epstein's departure was nothing compared to the December 21 revelation that Johnny Damon was going to sign with the Yankees as a free agent.

Johnny Damon, the noted center fielder, leadoff hitter, ALCS and World Series hero, and author—in pinstripes. Just like the bad old days.

The announcement that Damon was going to the Yankees was so shocking and so distressing, that the Red Sox called a press conference at Fenway Park to explain what did not happen. It was the first press conference in franchise history called to talk about a non-signing instead of a signing.

Naturally, there had to be a scapegoat. Only a few reasonable fans understood that baseball is a game in name only and a business in reality, and that whatever happened during Damon's free agency, it was all about the money. Otherwise, it was all about the Red Sox being too cheap or too stupid to re-sign their center fielder, or it was all about Damon being just another ungrateful, greedy, soon-to-be-more-overpaid star.

In Major League Baseball, the money never makes any sense to anyone in the outside world. What's the difference between $10 million and $12 million a year, anyway? Only the federal government could find a way to go broke with paychecks like that. In Major League Baseball, though, salary is how players compare themselves to their peers. If you hit .300 and I hit .290, but I make $12 million and you make $11 million, I'm better than you.

So for all of his good humor, good nature, wide grins, home runs, and stolen bases, Damon was no different than anybody else in his profession. And as much as he said he loved playing in Boston and the fans there, it did come down to money.

The Sox had paid him $31 million for the four seasons from 2002 to 2005. They were offering him about $40 million for the next four seasons, while New York wound up signing him for $52 million for four seasons.

Neither the Red Sox nor Damon looked good as the story of his defection began to fall into place. The Sox claimed that Damon never gave them a chance to match the Yankees' offer. Damon said that he could see the direction things were going and when New York made its bid, he simply had to take it.

In an interview with Boston TV station Channel 4, Damon said, "My message to Sox fans is I tried. I tried everything in my power. Unfortunately I know they are going to be upset. I'm always going to remember the good times, the World Series, the three out of four years we made the playoffs. I want them to know I appreciate them and I tried. I know they will continue to root for the Red Sox and they should. I'm going to try and win another World Series. That's what I have to do."

When he left, Damon was not the best player on the Red Sox, but he was the most popular. He had, in an offhand comment after the team clinched a playoff berth in 2004, created the "Idiots" persona, and he and Kevin Millar combined to turn it into a brand name. Future Hall of Famer Manny Ramirez was uncommunicative and David Ortiz had yet to fully grow into the "Big Papi" role, so Damon had become the voice and face of the organization.

He was a very different voice and face, which made him all the more popular. The Red Sox had long reflected their New England

Johnny Damon makes a running catch on a ball hit by Detroit Tigers' Bobby Higginson during the first inning at Fenway Park in Boston on Friday, August 27, 2004. (AP Photo/Winslow Townson)

heritage and dealt with their fans stoically and in cases like Nomar Garciaparra, Ted Williams, and Carl Yastrzemski, reluctantly. Damon loved interacting with fans, loved having his picture taken, loved being on TV, loved being quoted, and he looked like John the Baptist.

Who else would have told reporters at spring training in 2004 that he had added some weight during the off-season, and did it the old-fashioned way, by drinking beer? Who else would have said that he worked on his base running skills by going outside and running down his street next to cars as they pulled away from a stop sign? Who else would have eagerly embraced the idea that he position himself in center field so that when he made a catch, one of the signs out there looked like it said "Giant ass" and not "Giant Glass?"

What other player could write a tell-all book that often made him look bad, one entitled *Idiot—Beating the Curse and Enjoying the Game of Life*, and have it be a great commercial success?

This writer's wife, a Damon fan, bought the book and had me ask him to autograph it for her. He did so one day in Cleveland, asking me to leave the book on the chair in front of his locker and come back after batting practice. When I did come back, Damon was sitting in his chair, reading his own book, and laughing hysterically.

Damon was real. It was not an act, and what made it even better was that he could play. Damon played hard and he played hurt. He played when he shouldn't have in the 2003 postseason after suffering a serious concussion in a collision with infielder Damian Jackson, an injury that led him to his beer-fueled conditioning program that winter.

Damon had a terrible throwing arm and that reduced his value as a center fielder, but he could run, hit for average, and hit for more power than the standard leadoff man. More than anything, though, Red Sox fans identified Damon as the engine behind their team's World Series triumph in 2004. He was the man whose home runs beat the Yankees in Game 7 of the ALCS and who led off Game 4 of the World Series with a spirit-crushing home run in St. Louis.

About a year later he was gone, and his reasons didn't seem good enough.

"(The Yankees) showed they really wanted me," Damon told Channel 4. "I tried with Boston, waiting for them to step up, but unfortunately they didn't and now I'm headed to New York. They were coming after me aggressively. We know George Streinbrenner always wants to have the best players and he showed that.

"He and Brian Cashman came after me hard and now I'm a part of the Yankees and a great lineup. We're going to be tough to beat.

"I wasn't quite sure what happened, but I'm very excited. The (Yankees) players were calling me and trying to recruit me. They did a heck of a job doing it. You know, I'm with mixed emotions. I'm very happy starting a new career. I'm sad to say goodbye to some of the greatest fans in the world. Unfortunately they had to see this day, but it's time for me to move forward."

The deal with the Yankees meant it was time for both Damon and the Red Sox to move forward, and the passage of three seasons made it possible to look back at his defection to New York and see how it worked out for both sides.

Boston, which won one World Series during Damon's four years with the team, won another one without him, three seasons after he left. The Sox tried to replace Damon in center with Coco Crisp, but Crisp was disappointing. Rookie Jacoby Ellsbury was as fast as Damon, maybe faster, was a little better defensively, and had surprising pop in his bat. Ellsbury showed signs of growing into being Damon on the field, but was never going to be him off the field.

In New York, Damon played just about as advertised. His poor throwing arm was a problem at Yankee Stadium, so he was moved to left field for a while. Damon was banged up a lot, as he was in Boston, but played through the injuries, as he did in Boston.

The Yankees, though, didn't win a World Series in Damon's first three years in the Bronx. They didn't even go to one, and in 2008, the team failed to make the playoffs for the first time in 12 years.

Comparing Damon's performances in Boston and New York is interesting. In his first three seasons with the Red Sox, he batted .288, and averaged 115 runs, 75 RBIs, 27 steals, 34 doubles, 8 triples, and 15 home runs a year. In his first three seasons with the Yankees, Damon batted .286 and averaged 101 runs, 71 RBIs, 27 steals, 30 doubles, 4 triples, and 18 homers a year.

For Damon, the move to New York worked out financially and he maintained a solid level of play, although age seemed to be catching up with him a bit. For the Red Sox, they won without him and saved some money, and in the long term opened up an outfield spot for Ellsbury.

In the end, the Red Sox's management weren't cheapskates and Damon wasn't a traitor. They were both just businessmen, and his defection to the Yankees was baseball business as usual.

CHAPTER 16

THE GREATEST
SOX COMEBACK

The greatest comeback in baseball history is the Red Sox's return from a three games to zero deficit to beat the Yankees in the 2004 ALCS, and that is an undeniable fact. It had never been done before and the words "unprecedented" and "greatest" have a pretty strong connection.

But what about the team's best-ever comeback in one game? Boston trailed the Yankees by a run going into the bottom of the ninth in Game 4 of that historic '04 ALCS and won in extra innings. It was a dramatic comeback, but that kind of thing happens almost once a night somewhere during the course of a Major League Baseball season.

What then, would be the best comeback in Red Sox history—the come-from-behind-to-win-a-game-that-seemed-unwinnable-type of comeback? Every generation of Sox teams has its own greatest comeback, and every generation of Sox fans has a game like that to rally around. A few, however, and one in particular, stand out above the rest.

On Oct. 16, 2008, Boston trailed the Rays 7–0 with two out in the bottom of the seventh in Game 5 of the ALCS at Fenway Park and rallied to win, 8–7. At the time, the Red Sox also trailed in the series 3–1, and by virtue of the victory, kept their season alive and eventually went to seven games before losing that ALCS.

The 1967 Sox came back from an 8–0 deficit to beat the Angels 9–8 in the second game of a doubleheader at Fenway Park on August 20, 1967, and a case can be made for Boston's in Game 4 of the 2004 ALCS simply on long-term significance. For bewildering, illogical, and stunning drama, nothing beats the comebacks authored by Red Sox teams on Father's Day 1961, and Mother's Day 2007, and it is doubtful that anything will ever beat that Father's Day game.

On June 18, 1961, Boston played the expansion Washington Senators in a doubleheader at Fenway Park, and with two out in the bottom of the ninth of the first game, was losing by a score of 12–5. From seven runs down and one out left in the game—the Red Sox won, 13–12.

How did something like that ever happen?

It was a rather typical Fenway game through eight innings. The Senators built a 7–5 lead, doing a lot of their damage against Boston starter Ike Delock with a four-run rally in the fifth inning. Delock was relieved by Billy Muffett, who kept Washington in check heading into the ninth inning.

Senators manager Mickey Vernon, the former Red Sox first baseman, went almost all the way with the aptly named Carl "Stubby" Mathias, a lefty who stood less than 6' tall but weighed more than 200 pounds. It was Mathias' first start of his second and final season in the major leagues; his career record was 0–2. Had his bullpen been able to hold a seven-run lead, Mathias would have had at least one big-league win.

He helped expand his lead from two runs to seven by leading off the top of the ninth with a single. Muffett struck out Coot Veal then gave up a double to former Boston shortstop Billy Klaus, and manager Mike Higgins yanked Muffett in favor of lefty Ted Wills. Wills gave up a single and a walk before facing ex-Boston outfielder Willie Tasby who hit a grand slam to make it 12–5.

That would have been enough to send most of the fans home except that, in 1961, teams still played authentic doubleheaders in which ticketholders watched two games for the price of one. So, there were still plenty of people in the seats when the Red Sox came up in the last of the ninth.

Mathias began the inning by getting Vic Wertz to ground out. Then Don Buddin, who had homered earlier, hit a single, and Billy Harrell, batting for eventual winning pitcher Wills, struck out. Two outs, one

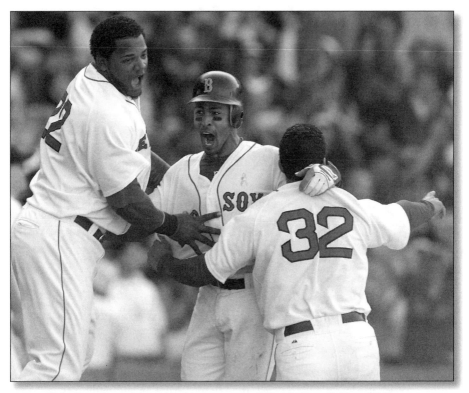

Julio Lugo (center) is mobbed by teammates Wily Mo Pena (left) and J.C. Romero (32) after Lugo's misplayed ground ball scored the winning run in the ninth inning of Boston's 6–5 win over the Baltimore Orioles in a baseball game at Fenway Park in Boston on Sunday, May 13, 2007. The Red Sox scored six runs in the ninth inning to win. (AP Photo/Winslow Townson)

on, still 12–5 Senators. Chuck Schilling and Carroll Hardy then both singled, driving in Buddin. Gary Geiger walked, Vernon finally came out and got Mathias, bringing in (there's a theme here) former Red Sox pitcher Dave Sisler to face Jackie Jensen.

Sisler walked Jensen then Frank Malzone. That made it a 12–8 game with the bases loaded for catcher Jim Pagliaroni, whose grand slam into the screen above the Green Monster tied it up. Sisler stayed in for one more batter, Wertz again, who walked. Marty Kutyna came in to face Buddin and the Sox shortstop singled again, sending Wertz to second. Higgins sent in Pete Runnels to run for Wertz and sent up Russ Nixon to pinch-hit for the pinch-hitting Harrell.

His ground ball somehow eluded the glove of Washington second baseman Chuck Cottier and Runnels scored the winning run. Boston 13, Washington 12.

I remember watching the game on TV and decided to try to track down some of the key participants and see if they remembered it which, of course, they did.

Sisler, a tall, scholarly Princeton alum who was the son of Hall of Famer George Sisler, took the loss. "It was the lowlight of my career," he said from St. Louis, where he was a prosperous stockbroker. "I remember that it was so bad that, between games of the doubleheader, two little girls sent me a note in the clubhouse saying how bad they felt for me."

"Every time I see Chuck (Cottier), I remind him," said Nixon, who later became a major league manager. "The thing about that inning was, sure, nobody expects to come back from seven runs down, but in those years, with the kind of explosive teams we had, all kinds of things happened at Fenway Park."

Pagliaroni's grand slam was the key to everything, and only part of a Bobby Thomson weekend. In the second game of the doubleheader, Pagliaroni hit a game-ending homer in the last of the thirteenth to give the Sox a 6–5 victory. On the day before the doubleheader, he hit a pinch home run as rookie pitcher Galen Cisco earned his first big-league win.

The memory of that comeback never left Sisler. "I felt so badly about what happened," he said, "that shortly after that, they were picking the All-Star Team, and they had to pick at least one player from each team and they had asked Dick Donovan from ours, but he was hurt—so they asked me instead.

"Well, they were gonna have a game in Boston (there were two All-Star Games in 1961) and I told them there was no way I would go back to Boston as an All-Star after what happened, that I wouldn't go until I deserved it." Sisler never was an All-Star, and all because of the greatest comeback in Red Sox history.

* * *

The Mother's Day comeback was on May 13, 2007, in the last game of a series with the Orioles and the third game of a 10-game homestand. Boston had hammered Baltimore pitching for 13 runs the day before, but on this afternoon, Orioles' starter Jeremy Guthrie completely dominated Sox batters, holding them to three harmless hits through eight innings.

Baltimore took a 5–0 lead into the bottom of the ninth and Guthrie got Julio Lugo to ground out to lead it off. Next up was Coco Crisp and he hit a high foul ball barely fair near home plate that catcher Ramon Hernandez dropped for an error.

With that, Orioles manager Sam Perlozzo took out Guthrie even though he had thrown just 91 pitches. "I'm glad he got taken out," Sox first baseman Kevin Youkilis said, "the way he was pitching."

"Me and Tim Wakefield looked at each other on the bench in the ninth inning when they took Guthrie out," said Josh Beckett who was going to be the losing pitcher. "We said, 'We're going to win this game.' We both believed it."

David Ortiz greeted reliever Danys Baez with a double to drive in Crisp. Wily Mo Pena singled Ortiz to third and Chris Ray came on to pitch. He walked J.D. Drew to load the bases and Youkilis to drive in the second run. Jason Varitek doubled in two more runs and it was a one-run game, 5–4.

Eric Hinske was intentionally walked to load the bases, then Alex Cora hit a grounder that resulted in a force play at home, giving Baltimore its second out of the inning. Back up to the plate again, Lugo hit a grounder wide of first base; he beat it out for an infield hit to make it 5–5, and as he did, Ray failed to catch Kevin Millar's throw to the bag and Hinske scored the winning run.

Had Baltimore won the game, it would have been 19–19. Instead, the loss sent the Orioles into a tailspin that cost Perlozzo his job a little more than a month later. The soon-to-be-former manager defended his decision to lift Guthrie, saying, "We were pretty much giving him an opportunity—if he could go 1–2–3—to stay in the ballgame. It was unfortunate that (Crisp) got on the way he did, but at that point, I thought we had our fresh arms out there, and I didn't want anything to get out of hand. Obviously, it didn't work."

Not for Baltimore, but it worked big-time for the Red Sox, who added an unforgettable chapter to their comeback history.

* * *

The ALCS comeback of 2008 saw Boston come from behind to win from the second-largest deficit in postseason history. The largest deficit overcome was during Game 4 of the 1929 World Series at Philly's Shibe Park. The Philadelphia Athletics were trailing the Cubs 8–0 going into the bottom of the seventh and scored 10 runs in that half-inning to win, 10–8. That victory gave the A's a three games to one lead in the series and they won the next game to clinch it.

What was so remarkable about the Red Sox's 2008 comeback was the nature of the turnaround in such a short span. After winning the first game of the series and losing the second one in extra innings at Tampa Bay, Boston came back to Fenway Park and did nothing right for 24 straight innings. They lost 9–1, then 13–4, and going into the bottom of the seventh on October 16, the Sox had been outscored 29–5 in the three games at Fenway.

In that Game 5, Rays manager Joe Maddon lifted Scott Kazmir after six innings with the lefty having pitched his team to a 7–0 lead. Kazmir was not tiring—he retired the last nine batters he faced, four on strikeouts. Maddon went to Grant Balfour for the seventh and the first batter he faced was shortstop Jed Lowrie batting left-handed, by far his weaker side. Lowrie stroked a double to right—a ball that would have been a home run in any other park—to give the Sox their first extra-base hit of the night.

Lowrie was still at second with two out when Coco Crisp singled to left, moving Lowrie to third. Dustin Pedroia's single to right made it 7–1 and brought up David Ortiz, who had done nothing offensively in the series. Maddon kept righty Balfour in the game to pitch to Ortiz, and Ortiz delivered his biggest hit of 2008, sending a three-run homer into the right-field corner to make it 7–4, and suddenly a winnable game.

"I believe it was," replied Crisp when asked if that homer was the turning point. "I believe that when Papi connected with it, that was when everyone thought, everyone on our team, all of the fans, that, hey—this might happen."

In the eighth, J.D. Drew hit a two-run homer with nobody out and it was 7–6. Mark Kotsay doubled with two out, then scored the tying run on Crisp's sharp single to right. The ball was hit hard enough to make it a gamble to send Kotsay home, but Rays right fielder Gabe Gross slipped as he made the throw and Kotsay scored easily.

With two out and nobody on base in the ninth, Kevin Youkilis hit a slow grounder down the third base line that Rays third baseman Evan Longoria made a nice play on, then threw away to allow Youkilis to get to second. The Rays intentionally walked Jason Bay to force a lefty-lefty matchup with Drew and reliever J.P. Howell, but Drew won the battle by lining a shot over Gross' head in right to send Youkilis home with the winning run.

"No question. Without a doubt," Lowrie said reflecting on the suggestion that the game was one of the best baseball games he had ever played in. "I've had a couple of walk-off hits this year, but to be part of a game like that is a feeling that will stay with me, I'm sure, probably forever.

"You know, while it was all going on, it was surreal. It was hard to believe it was actually happening. And then it was over, and the reaction was like, 'Hey—we just won that game.'"

Game 6 went to Boston 4–2, but the Sox were shut down by Matt Garza in Game 7 at Tampa Bay and the Rays went to the World Series.

DUSTIN PEDROIA

During the damply joyous celebration in the Red Sox clubhouse after Boston had beaten the Cleveland Indians in Game 7 of the 2007 ALCS, general manager Theo Epstein was asked if—now, be honest Theo—the Sox had projected second baseman Dustin Pedroia to be as good as he turned out to be. "Well, maybe not THIS good," Epstein conceded, just before getting another champagne shower.

In that Game 7, an 11–2 victory, Pedroia had gone 3-for-5 with a home run, three runs scored, and five driven in. It was a long, long way from where his career had been just a year before when there was some question as to whether or not Boston might have made a mistake in taking him with its first pick—a second-round choice—in the 2004 draft.

Pedroia was called up from Pawtucket on August 21, 2006, and made his major-league debut the next night playing shortstop, which was in line with how some past Sox stars began their careers out of position—Nomar Garciaparra debuted at second base and Ted Williams in right field. Pedroia got his first hit in his second at-bat, but in general, his first taste of the big leagues was disappointing; he hit just .191 in 31 games.

When Jim Rice came up to the majors for the first time late in 1974, he hit .269 in 24 games and had just one home run. Fred Lynn, on the other hand, was also a late-season callup in '74 and batted .419 with two homers. Garciaparra hit merely .241 in September 1996 before his amazing rookie season of 1997, but Jacoby Ellsbury hit .353 with three homers and nine stolen bases after he came up late in the 2007 season, so there was just no projecting how well a young player would do in the long term from his early numbers.

In Pedroia's case, though, his 2006 problems continued in 2007. One month into the season, he was batting only .182 and manager Terry Francona, while telling inquiring reporters that Pedroia was just too good a player to give up on, had begun alternating him at second base with veteran Alex Cora. In fact, the Red Sox opened a series in Minnesota on May 4 and Cora was at second with Pedroia on the bench; to that point in his career, Pedroia was hitting .180.

Dustin Pedroia, left, throws to first base to complete the double play after forcing out New York Yankees' Bobby Abreu (53) during fifth inning baseball action on Wednesday, Aug. 29, 2007, at Yankee Stadium in New York. The Yankees' Alex Rodriguez was out at first. (AP PHOTO/ FRANK FRANKLIN II)

Throughout his early offensive difficulties, Pedroia played a top-notch second base. He had an uncanny ability to make diving stops, particularly to his left, and somehow wind up with the ball in the webbing of his glove. He was fearless to the point of being confrontational when turning double plays and had a strong, accurate arm.

The player who wound up winning American League Rookie of the Year honors in 2007 was born in Minneapolis the day after having that night of May 4 off.

Batting in the ninth spot, Pedroia went 2-for-2 with a double on May 5. He went 3-for-4 with two doubles the next game, then had consecutive 2-for-4 games. It added up to 9-for-14 in four games, his average went from .180 to .267, and Pedroia was off and running never to look back.

The sudden surge that began in Minnesota was the first glimpse at just how hot Pedroia could get with the bat. From May 23 to June 3 he was 19-for-34, his average went from .260 to .336, and he was never under .300 again. Pedroia wound up with 165 hits and a .317 average and was an overwhelming choice as Rookie of the Year, Boston's first since Garciaparra in 1997. He continued to hit through the 2008 season, and eventually just fell just two points shy of winning the American League batting title. He followed up his Rookie of the Year Award by being named the American League Most Valuable Player.

The media guides list Pedroia at 5'9", but he is shorter than that, perhaps 5'7". He has an uppercut swing that makes most scientific hitting coaches cringe, and he probably swings way too hard to make consistent contact. He plays with a chip on his shoulder and carries that attitude into the clubhouse—even into his frequent cribbage games with Francona. At the same time, Pedroia is so genuinely affable that he is one of the most popular players on the team.

Baseball is a game of surprises, most of them unpleasant. Dustin Pedroia surprised the Red Sox, at least a little. They thought he'd be good, but didn't think he would be the next coming of Bobby Doerr.

* * *

The 1967 season was filled with games like the Red Sox's comeback to beat the Angels in the second game of that August 20 Sunday doubleheader at Fenway, a doubleheader played two days after Jack Hamilton hit Tony Conigliaro in the eye with a fastball that ended his season, and to a large extent, his career.

On Sunday, California—that's what the Angels were called at that particular stage of their American League lives—built an 8–0 lead off Boston starter Dave Morehead and reliever Dan Osinski. It was 8–0 early, though, so the Sox had time to come back, and it started with Reggie Smith's solo homer in the last of the fourth. In the fifth, Carl Yastrzemski hit a three-run home run off California starter Jim McGlothlin to make it 8–4; after McGlothlin gave up a single to George Scott, Hamilton made an appearance in relief.

He got Smith to ground out to end the inning, but the first three Boston batters reached in the sixth to load the bases and Hamilton was gone from the game in favor of Minnie Rojas. Dalton Jones' double, a sacrifice fly, and a base hit by Jerry Adair tied the game at 8–8 before the inning was finally over.

Adair led off the bottom of the eighth with his second home run of the season, a bomb into the screen in left-center, and the Red Sox had a 9–8 lead, one they preserved even though the Angels had men at second and third with nobody out in top of the ninth and the bases loaded with two out.

It was that kind of game for Boston and that kind of year.

CHAPTER 17

JOHNNY PESKY

Nobody has done more, on and off the field, or become more of a symbol for the Red Sox franchise than Johnny Pesky. And for that matter, no one has ever been the subject of more incorrect mythology.

Pesky held the ball. Pesky hit one off the right-field foul pole to win a game for Mel Parnell. Neither thing ever happened, but fans talk about them today like they were as much fact as the Battle of Fort Sumter or the Hurricane of 1938.

Pesky was one of the first products of Tom Yawkey's new farm system, a shortstop from Portland, Oregon, who could bunt, hit-and-run, poke singles all over the place, and take over at shortstop for the aging Joe Cronin, who had no range and never was that good defensively, anyway. After a quick rise through the Red Sox minors, Pesky made his debut on April 14, 1942, Opening Day that season.

As a rookie, Pesky had 205 hits and batted .331. He was the perfect complement to a Boston batting order that already included a young Ted Williams, a young Dominic DiMaggio, and Bobby Doerr, who was entering his sixth major league season in 1942 but was only 24.

Pesky's great rookie season was followed by three years in the military. His return in 1946 was like that of Williams and DiMaggio—it looked like he had never left. Pesky's bat at the top of the batting order and steady glove at short helped the Red Sox to their first American League pennant since 1918. And, of course, their first World Series appearance, which is where the myths begin.

Held the Ball?

The Red Sox and Cardinals were tied at three games apiece when they met for Game 7 at Sportsman's Park in St. Louis on October 15. They were not only tied 3–3 in games, they were also tied 3–3 on the scoreboard going into the bottom of the eighth. Cleanup batter Enos Slaughter led off the eighth with a single, but the Cardinals were not able to advance him into scoring position. So he was still there when left fielder Harry Walker came up to face Boston pitcher Bob Klinger. Walker, a left-handed batter, had been the Cardinals' best batter during the World Series and was 6-for-16 (.375) as he stood in against Klinger.

Walker lined a double to left-center—many accounts of the play say that Slaughter scored from first on a single, but he did not. With two out, Slaughter took off on contact. Red Sox center fielder Leon Culberson tracked the ball down and threw it in to Pesky, the cutoff man in short left-center field. Pesky turned and threw home to catcher Roy Partee, but Slaughter beat the throw to score what turned out to be the winning run of the World Series.

It was a complex play and a number of things could have gone wrong for either team. They went wrong for Boston, and Pesky has been blamed for holding on to the ball after getting it from Culberson, thus giving Slaughter enough time to score.

There is film of the play. It is better quality than the hazy image of Babe Ruth waving his arms around on the "called shot" in 1932, but as is typical of things from the pre-videotape days, a bit inconclusive. Think of the footage from Bobby Thomson's home run—are those fans *really* cheering that home run? Or of Ted Williams' homer in his final time up in the majors—the ball leaves Williams' bat, then disappears, then a ball lands in the Boston bullpen. Same swing?

The film of what has come to be called Slaughter's "Mad Dash" is slightly disconnected and disorienting, but it does show one thing very clearly. Pesky didn't hold the ball. It shows him getting Culberson's throw, turning towards the infield, and throwing towards home plate.

Boston Red Sox great Johnny Pesky hits while helping out with fielding drills at the team's spring training baseball practice in Fort Myers, Florida, on Friday, March 9, 2007. Pesky, 87, made his major league debut in 1942. (AP PHOTO/ CHARLES KRUPA)

Was there a hesitation in there somewhere? Yes, but it was slight, less than a second. As for actually holding the ball while Slaughter was headed for the plate—that did not happen, and nobody watching the film of the play can possibly come to that conclusion.

One problem is that after the game, Pesky accepted the blame for what happened. He was quoted as saying, "I'm the goat. I never expected he'd try to score. I couldn't hear anybody hollering at me above the noise of the crowd. I gave Slaughter at least six strides with the delay. I know I could have nailed him if I suspected he would try for the plate. I'm the goat; make no mistake about it."

Six strides? Slaughter was really motoring, so six strides would have been worth probably between 20 and 25 feet of base path. There is no way that Pesky's slight hesitation, if it happened, gave Slaughter that much extra.

In his book, *The Boston Red Sox World Series Encyclopedia*, Bill Nowlin transcribed Mel Allen's radio description of the play and there is no mention of Pesky holding the ball. Allen's account: "There goes Slaughter. The ball is swung on...there's a line drive going into left-center field; it's in there for a base hit. Culberson fumbles the ball momentarily and Slaughter charges around second, heads for third. Pesky heads into short left field to take the relay from Culberson, and here comes Slaughter rounding third. He's going to try for home—here comes the throw and it's not in time. Slaughter scores."

Allen says that Culberson bobbled the ball, not that Pesky held it.

Years later Pesky saw things differently than he had right after Game 7 and told Dan Shaughnessy for his book, *The Curse of the Bambino*, "No one dreamed that Slaughter would try to score. I'm out in short left-center field. It was late in the afternoon and, Christ, when I picked him up he was about 20 feet from home plate. I'd have needed a rifle to get him."

In the *Worcester Telegram* account of Game 7, reporter Roy Mumpton said that Pesky took two or three strides towards the infield before letting the ball go and clearly felt that the Boston shortstop had held it too long. Mumpton quoted manager Joe Cronin as putting his arm around Pesky in the clubhouse and saying, "Forget it," then adding for reporters, "The less said about that play, the better. Pesky is a great ballplayer and has a great career ahead of him."

The film footage of the play is like the Zapruder film, in a sense—every viewer can come away with a different assessment. The eyewitness conclusion in St. Louis that afternoon was that Pesky held the ball for too long. The harder evidence is that he did not and never had a real chance at getting Slaughter.

"Pesky's Pole"

For most Red Sox fans, the right-field foul pole at Fenway has been known as Pesky's Pole for as long as anyone has been going to games there. But why?

The accepted version of the facts is that former Sox lefty Mel Parnell was responsible for the nickname when he was a Boston broadcaster in the 1960s. Parnell related how Pesky once hit a home run off the right-field pole to win a game for him.

That never happened.

Pesky and Parnell were teammates on the Red Sox from the start of the 1947 season until Pesky was traded to Detroit during the '52 campaign. In all that time, Pesky hit just nine home runs and only three of those homers were hit at Fenway Park. Only one of them was hit in a game that Parnell appeared in—the second game of a doubleheader against the Tigers on June 11, 1950.

Boston lost that game 9–6 in 14 innings. Pesky's home run was hit in the first inning and was described in the newspaper accounts as a towering drive into the right-field seats. The foul pole was never mentioned. In his entire major league career, Pesky hit six home runs at Fenway Park. Maybe one or two of them hit the right-field foul pole, but Mark Bellhorn did that, too.

It is alliterative—Pesky's Pole—but probably not very accurate. And, like the myth of him holding the ball in Game 7 of the 1946 World Series, it is not likely to go away.

CHAPTER 18

THE GREATEST CATCH

When the ball left Joe Morgan's bat for the far reaches of Fenway Park's right-field corner, the only question seemed to be how many bases would the Reds second baseman get out of it? It looked like a home run, depending on what track the ball took towards the foul pole. If not that, then a ground-rule double, or it could rattle around on the warning track while the speedy Morgan zipped around the bases for a triple.

Whatever the options, they were bad ones for the Red Sox, save for an unexpected one—Boston right fielder Dwight Evans caught the ball, turning Morgan's potential go-ahead hit into a double play that ended the top of the eleventh inning in Game 6 of the Red Sox–Reds World Series in 1975.

Evans, stumbling and leaping at the same time, has been immortalized on videotape with that play, often called the greatest catch in Fenway Park history. Greatest catch? Of that World Series sure, and maybe even of the 1970s, but not the greatest, nor even most dramatic or significant one ever made at Fenway Park.

There is a long list of candidates. There is no ballpark in the major leagues that lends itself to great outfield plays more than Fenway Park. It has short fences all the way from the right-field foul pole to the end of the bullpens in right-center. It has the curve of the right-field corner and the unique exclamation point of the triangle in right-center. Anywhere along those lines, outfielders can snatch potential home runs out of the crowd, turn triples into outs, or tumble over fences.

Outfielder Bob Zupcic made the third-greatest catch in Fenway history when he deprived Tigers catcher Mickey Tettleton of a home run on September 13, 1992.
(AP Photo)

Identifying one particular play as the greatest catch ever made at Fenway Park is highly subjective, but when the topic is broached to anybody who was around the Red Sox in the 1960s, the vote is unanimous—it was made by Indians right fielder Al Luplow on the afternoon of June 27, 1963.

The circumstances: Boston trailed the Indians 6–3 with one out in the bottom of the eighth. Luplow was the Cleveland right fielder, having entered the game in the sixth inning as a defensive replacement for Gene Green. The Red Sox had Lu Clinton at third base and Dick Stuart at first for future Hall of Fame manager Dick Williams, who was playing third base that day.

Facing side-arming Ted Abernathy, Williams stroked a long drive to deep right-center. Luplow, a running back at Michigan State in his college days, took off after the ball as soon as it was hit. He and the baseball arrived at the Red Sox bullpen at just about the same time. Luplow, going full speed, lept after the ball and hit the fence with his knee just as he made the catch on the backhand—the ball was several feet deep into the airspace of the Boston bullpen.

The Indians right fielder then tumbled out of sight. Second-base umpire Joe Paparella raced out towards the Boston pen, waited a bit, then gave the out sign. Clinton tagged at third base and scored and Stuart moved up to second, but so what? Instead of having a game-tying three-run homer, Williams had a sacrifice fly and the game was 6–4, not 6–6. It ended as a 6–4 Cleveland victory.

Boston manager Johnny Pesky raced onto the field to argue the call, telling Paparella that the ball was out of play when Luplow caught it, not that Luplow didn't catch it. Paparella knew that Luplow had made the catch, he said, by the simple fact that had he not, the Red Sox bullpen would have reacted by celebrating.

Indeed, nobody tried to say Luplow didn't make the catch. In Roger Birtwell's account of the game and catch, in the next day's *Boston Globe*, an unidentified member of the Sox pen was quoted as saying, "As Luplow went down sidewise, he tucked the ball close to his body. He tumbled on his shoulder and head like a football player. And he was up on his feet fast.

"It was a wonderful catch, but that ball was beyond the fence and over the bullpen when he caught it."

That point, however, was irrelevant. Players have always been allowed to reach over fences and catch balls. The key point isn't where the ball is, it is where the player is—and if any part of his body is still within the playing field, it is a legitimate catch. Which is what Paparella, in his 18th season as a major league umpire, ruled.

Pesky protested the game when he could not get Paparella to change the call, then later dropped the protest. Years later, Pesky lamented that his relievers didn't think fast enough and act as though Luplow had dropped it, adding, "I told Al Lakeman, the bullpen coach, that at least somebody should have tossed a ball in the air so it looked like Luplow dropped it."

For all of his many, and legendary, baseball accomplishments, Williams enjoyed talking about two events more than anything else—

the Impossible Dream Sox of 1967 that he managed to the pennant and Luplow's catch. In 1985, Williams talked to writer Jay Feldman of *Sports Illustrated* and said, "Al used to play hell-bent for election. He was a hustler. He'd run through a brick wall to make a play."

For the same article, Paparella recalled Luplow's catch by saying, "I was between 50 and 60 feet away. Luplow's feet were still in the playing territory when he caught the ball. He had possession of the ball after he fell into the bullpen, and he came up with it. It was an out. There was no question about it."

Luplow was not a great college football player, but good enough to make a Big 10 roster, and he was a high school All-American in his hometown of Saginaw, Michigan. Oddly, the Boston pitcher who might have gotten a win that day if Luplow had not caught Williams' fly ball, was Dick Radatz, a teammate of Luplow's on the Michigan State baseball team.

Luplow remembered his play this way when talking to Feldman, "It was in between a line drive and a fly ball. I kept getting closer and closer to it, and I said to myself, 'I gotta catch this ball.' I felt the warning track, so I was definitely aware of the wall. But I guess I'd just made up my mind to catch the ball. It was actually over the fence when I caught it, and I just barely touched the fence with my right knee going over.

"After I caught the ball, I said 'uh-oh.' If I'd kept going face first, I would have really hurt myself. I think my football background helped me because I tucked my left shoulder and rolled, and fortunately all I did was spike myself on the right knee."

Luplow then held the ball up to show that he had made the catch and transferred it to center fielder Willie Kirkland, who threw it back to the infield to see if the Indians could turn a double play, but Clinton and Stuart had both tagged up legally.

"I sure wouldn't ever do it again," Luplow said. "I could easily have broken my neck. I must have put those guys in the bullpen in shock."

It turned out that Luplow's catch put the entire Red Sox team in shock. Going into that game the Sox, with rookie manager Pesky at the helm, were off to their best start in years. They were 10 games over .500 and just 2½ games out of first place. Starting with the Luplow loss, Boston went 1–5 in a span of six games and fell to 5½ gamed behind.

The Sox-Indians game of June 27 was not televised and there was no film taken of Luplow's catch, but for those who where there and saw it first hand, or were involved in the play, there has never been another one like it.

If Luplow's catch is the greatest in the history of Fenway Park, it is not the only great one. Evans' catch on Morgan is a Hall of Fame catch because of the circumstances, but it probably ranks down the list a bit in terms of pure athleticism.

* * *

The runner-up to Luplow is Harry Hooper, with another play that was never caught on film or videotape because it happened in 1912, the year that Fenway Park opened.

The Red Sox won the American League pennant handily in 1912 and played the National League champion New York Giants in the World Series. The second game, played at Fenway Park, went 11 innings and ended in a 6–6 tie with the game eventually called because of darkness. That made it an eight-game Series, with the eighth and deciding game played at Fenway on October 16.

The Series was tied, three games apiece, and the Giants had a 1–0 lead when Larry Doyle came up with one out and nobody on base in the top of the fifth. Even before it was remodeled by Tom Yawkey, Fenway Park's right-field fence was a long way from home plate and for the World Series, the Red Sox installed temporary bleachers in the outfield in right.

Doyle launched a pitch from Red Sox starter Smoky Joe Wood in the direction of those temporary bleachers. Accounts of the game say that Hooper, eventually in the Hall of Fame, turned his back to the plate as soon as the ball was hit and headed for where he thought it would land. Hooper and the ball arrived at the fence—three feet high—in front of the temporary bleachers, and Hooper reached in about three rows deep to catch it.

Hooper did not just catch Doyle's potential home run—he caught the ball barehanded and with his back to the plate. The catch saved a run for sure and thus saved the World Series for Boston. The Sox managed to tie the game at 1–1 and win it 3–2 in 10 innings. Without Hooper robbing Doyle, Boston never would have gotten it to extra innings and would have lost the first World Series ever played at Fenway Park, not won it.

* * *

The third greatest catch in Fenway history was also by a Red Sox player, Bob Zupcic. It had even less significance than Luplow's, coming on September 13, 1992, a season that saw Boston finish 16 games under .500. The game on September 13 was against the Tigers and the Red Sox's 7–2 loss was the second in a four-game losing streak.

Zupcic's catch was also, of all the memorable Fenway catches, the most unique. There are ballparks all over baseball where players can climb fences and dive into crowds, but only in Fenway, with its triangle in right center field, can a player catch a ball that had already traveled some 20 feet over the fence.

Boston was behind 6–1 when Tigers catcher Mickey Tettleton, a switch hitter, came up to lead off in the top of the seventh. Tettleton was hitting left handed with rookie right hander Paul Quantrill on the mound for the Red Sox. Quantrill was prone to giving up home runs, and Tettleton sent a towering drive towards the Boston bullpen.

Center fielder Zupcic got a good jump on the ball. He was one of the Sox's fastest players and zipped back to the center-field wall some 420 feet—the furthest point in the ballpark—from home plate. Tettleton's blast cleared the bullpen fence easily and headed towards the back wall of the Boston pen.

From his spot in the triangle, though, Zupcic climbed up onto the sideways bullpen fence, reached over the railing, and caught

Tettleton's potential home run. It was an amazing bit of quick thinking, as well as ability. Nobody had ever seen a home run taken away in that manner—by an outfielder reaching sideways into the bullpen. But it was a legal catch, and Tettleton was out. *Boston Globe* columnist Bob Ryan, in attendance at the Sunday afternoon game, said it was, "As good a center field grab as I've seen in 41 years of Fenway watching."

* * *

The catch Bo Jackson made for the Royals at Fenway on Saturday afternoon, April 22, 1989, was a football player's catch, much as Luplow's was 26 years earlier. Boston catcher Rich Gedman was the leadoff man in the bottom of the fourth and smashed a pitch from Kansas City starter Mark Gubicza towards the gap in left-center field.

The ball was hit on a hard line; it was going to either hit the base of the Green Monster or bounce in front of it and then off. Either way, it looked like a double, even for the slow-footed Gedman. Except that somehow, Jackson raced over from left field and got to the ball. Diving to his left, straight out and parallel to the outfield grass, Jackson made the catch then skidded to a soft landing.

Said Boston manager Joe Morgan at the time, "I've never seen anything like it in 37 years of professional baseball."

* * *

On the night of July 29, 1997, Seattle right fielder Jay Buhner took a home run away from Scott Hatteberg on a play that reminded those with long memories of Luplow's catch, but it was not quite as spectacular, and it came in a game the Red Sox won.

Boston was up on the Mariners 4–0 behind the brilliant pitching of Tim Wakefield when Hatteberg came up to bat against Edwin Hurtado to lead off the bottom of the eighth. Hatteberg hit one to deep right-center and Buhner gauged where the ball might come down, then hustled back to brace himself against the fence in front of the Red

Sox bullpen. Using the top of the fence to push off, Buhner propelled himself into the air, caught Hatteberg's fly ball, then fell over into the bullpen and out of sight.

An instant later, Buhner was on his feet with the ball in his glove for an out.

Hatteberg was one of the few Boston players who didn't show a little grudging admiration for Buhner's play. Earlier in the season, in April, he had lost a home run when a ball he hit banged off a TV camera in center field and was ruled in play. So, he figured two lost home runs in the same season were a bit much. "I lead the league in lost homers," Hatteberg said. "He made a great catch and when he fell over, I hoped he dropped it, but I guess he didn't."

No, he didn't, as members of the Boston bullpen attested to.

"I had my eyes wide open and my mouth wide open," said closer Heathcliff Slocumb. "I couldn't believe it. It was the best catch I've ever seen." According to Jim Corsi, Sox relievers remained silent as they watched the play unfold. "It was a funny feeling," Corsi said. "I almost wanted to go over and high-five him."

Bullpen catcher Dana Levangie was warming up Butch Henry when the ball headed in his direction, so he got out of the way just before Buhner came over the fence. "The first thing I did was see if he was okay," Levangie said, "then see if he caught the ball."

And he did.

* * *

Next on the list is a catch that was extremely significant, and remains one of the most replayed ones ever made by a Boston outfielder. It is Tom Brunansky's sliding catch in right on a sinking line drive by White Sox shortstop Ozzie Guillen.

The Red Sox went into the night of October 3, 1990, with a one-game lead on the Blue Jays in the American League East title race, and one game left to play, the same as Toronto. Boston's magic number to win the division title outright was one. A Red Sox victory or Blue Jays' loss would do it. If the opposite happened, the teams would play off for first place in Toronto the next day.

Behind strong starting pitching by Mike Boddicker, Boston built an early 3–0 lead. Chicago got a run in the seventh to make it 3–1 and Red Sox manager Joe Morgan decided to bring in closer Jeff Reardon for the eighth inning.

Reardon got the White Sox in the eighth to keep it a 3–1 game, then began the top of the ninth by getting two very quick and easy outs. With everyone in Fenway Park on their feet preparing to celebrate the capture of the AL East title, Reardon gave up a two-out single to Sammy Sosa.

That brought Scott Fletcher to the plate as the potential tying run, but Fletcher wasn't much of a home-run threat and the lead seemed safe enough. Until Reardon hit Fletcher with a pitch—Rodney McCray ran for Fletcher—and suddenly the White Sox had fast men at first and second and the extremely dangerous Guillen up.

Guillen played the game the way he eventually managed it. He was completely unpredictable with a flair for the dramatic and loved the spotlight. Guillen was a hard batter to pitch to, since he sprayed the ball all over the field and could make good contact with pitches out of the strike zone. He could run, too, and historically had been a very difficult out for Boston pitchers.

Reardon was a strike thrower, which sometimes worked to his disadvantage, and he threw two quick strikes to Guillen, creating an unimaginable din in Fenway. And then Guillen lined the 0–2 pitch towards the right-field corner.

Red Sox fans had seen balls headed that way for decades and they knew what the outcome usually was. At the very least, it would be a double scoring one run and putting men at second and third. More likely, it would be a double and, with two out and two fast runners on, both would score to tie the game. If it got past Brunansky, who looked like he was going to try to catch it, then Guillen very likely would have an inside-the-park home run and the White Sox would have a 4–3 lead.

Brunansky did try to catch the ball and, sliding on the warning track in the direction of the right-field foul pole, made the play to end the game.

Not everybody was sure, though. As he made the catch, Brunansky slid out of sight of about half the fans in the ballpark and the entire Red Sox dugout. Right after the ball seemed to enter his glove, Brunansky reached behind himself to retrieve something, which could very well have been the ball, but turned out to be his hat. Brunansky then got to his feet and held his glove up with the ball in it and Boston had the AL East title.

After the game, Brunansky told reporters how close the ball was to landing fair. "It had to be inches," he said, "but I had made up my mind that, regardless, I was going for it."

The people who saw the play clearly knew Brunansky had caught the ball, but that wasn't everybody in the building. First-base umpire Tim McClelland had gone down the foul line to be in position to make the call, but before he could signal anything he was knocked over by a fan racing onto the field.

"I ran down the line," McClelland told Claire Smith of the *New York Times*, "so I could be in position to point fair. (Brunansky) started to jump up to show me he had possession. His hat came off—that's what he reached back to get. I couldn't make the out call because I was hit by a fan, but he had the ball in his glove. He ran in and handed it to me."

Chicago manager Jeff Torborg, in the third base dugout, was in perfect position to see the play and never even thought about arguing because he knew it was a legal catch. "I can't believe he caught the ball," Torborg said. "Nobody plays Ozzie Guillen that far over."

As the Red Sox and their fans were celebrating, the Blue Jays were playing the Orioles in Baltimore and about 10 minutes after Brunansky robbed Guillen to ensure the AL East title for his team, Toronto lost to the Orioles 3–2 making the great catch academic, but nonetheless remarkable.

* * *

Evans' catch was on October 21, 1975, and preserved the 6–6 tie that the Red Sox had forged on Bernie Carbo's pinch three-run homer in eighth inning.

Pete Rose led off the top of the 11th and Boston reliever Dick Drago hit him with a pitch—never a good way to start an inning, especially considering who the Reds had coming up after Rose: Ken Griffey, Joe Morgan, and Johnny Bench. Griffey bunted, but it wasn't a good one, and all he did was exchange places on first base with Rose. That brought up Morgan and his blast into the right-field corner.

Remembering the play years later for *Red Sox Legends* by Arcadia Publishing, Evans said, "I was actually, before that pitch...thinking if the ball is hit in the gap...I've got to go into the stands. Of course, I didn't end up doing that, but that's what went through my mind, and then when the ball was hit, I was actually prepared for it. It wasn't the best catch I ever made, but it was the most important catch I ever made.

"Usually when a left-hander hits the ball to right field, the ball hooks a little toward the right-field line, and when Joe Morgan hit this ball, I turned to my left and started running back at an angle, anticipating the ball hooking a little bit or curving toward the line.

"Well, as I get back, the ball was not curving at all but staying straight. So I actually caught the ball behind me, it was behind my head. Now, if you ever play catch with somebody, turn sideways and have them throw it on the other side of your head and try to catch it. You lose it for about three or four feet, and that's what happened in that play. So no one was happier than me to feel that ball go in my glove because I had lost it for that certain amount of time there."

Which explains why it seemed like Evans made the catch look harder than it was by leaping at the end. He had a few feet to go before being backed up against the low fence in the right-field corner, and even now, no matter how many times anyone looks at the replay, it is not clear if Morgan's ball would have been a home run or not. Reds bullpen catcher Bill Plummer said after the game that he thought it would have landed two rows deep into the seats.

Had Evans not caught it, the ball might have bounced into the stands for a ground rule double, moving Griffey over to third, but keeping it a 6–6 game. Had the ball stayed in play, it was at least a double and probably a triple, and Griffey would have undoubtedly scored the go-ahead run and Cincinnati would have won the World Series in six games.

Instead, Evans relayed the ball back to the infield, where shortstop Rick Burleson retrieved it and beat Griffey back to first base to complete the inning-ending double play. An inning later, Carlton Fisk hit one off the left-field foul pole to end what some fans still think was the greatest World Series game ever played.

* * *

In the first week of August 2002, Sox batters seemed to have gotten their signals crossed. They were supposed to hit the long ball; instead, they hit the ball to Long—Oakland center fielder Terrence Long—who kept catching it, costing Boston victories and at least one home run.

It took Manny Ramirez one extra swing to hit his 500th home run because of a catch Long made at Fenway Park on the night of August 7, 2002. It was another of those "taking it out of the bullpen" grabs and the best one of its kind seen since Zupcic's 10 years earlier.

Oakland had a 3–2 lead heading into the last of the ninth that evening with closer Billy Koch on the mound. With one out, Koch walked Johnny Damon then gave up a single to Trot Nixon. Boston had Nomar Garciaparra and Ramirez due up next, so the Fenway crowd was buzzing. Garciaparra struck out, however, leaving it up to Ramirez to keep the inning going and keep the Red Sox's comeback hopes alive. For a few seconds, it seemed as though he had done more than that.

Ramirez, whose true power always was to right-center field, smashed a high line drive in the direction of the Boston bullpen. Long galloped back to where it seemed the ball would leave the playing field, got there before the baseball did, leapt as high as he could and reached back to pull the would-be home run out of the bullpen, taking a game-ending three-run homer away from Ramirez.

When Long flashed the ball in his glove as he came back down to earth, he and Athletics right fielder Jermaine Dye celebrated together by collapsing in a heap on the outfield grass and the entire Oakland bench raced out to join them.

"Once I got close to the (warning) track," Long said, "I saw the ball was high enough, and I had a chance to slow down. I had a good bead on it."

The center fielder was asked if he thought it was his best catch ever and he replied, "Yes, considering the situation—last of the ninth, two outs, the game on the line. That's the best you can get."

Boston manager Grady Little said, "I thought it was gone because Manny has a way of hitting balls like that, that continue to carry. The kid made a great play out there. You have to give him credit. He caught that ball on a dead sprint."

Athletics manager Art Howe said that Long's play was, "as good as it gets. When (Ramirez) first hit it, I thought it would be a can 'o corn, but that son of a gun is so strong the ball just kept going and going. But what a catch. I don't know how he got there. Really, he hit the wall about the same time he caught the ball. I'm just thankful he held on. It was a miraculous catch—it was good TV."

* * *

The last entry on the unofficial list was a catch made by an opposing player who later carved out a notch in Red Sox history by hitting a home run on the first pitch he saw in the 2007 World Series, Bobby Kielty.

Kielty, whose family originally hailed from Fitchburg, Massachusetts, had just been traded from the Twins to the Blue Jays when Toronto arrived at Fenway Park for a four-game series right after the All-Star break in 2003. The Jays won the first two games, then the Sox took the third game and were looking for a split as they played on Sunday afternoon,

July 20. The odds were in their favor as Boston had Pedro Martinez on the mound opposed by Toronto's John "Way Back" Wasdin.

The Red Sox scored first on Kevin Millar's solo home run with one out in the second, then Trot Nixon followed him to the plate. It looked like back-to-back shots when Nixon lofted one to right, but the ball was hit high enough to allow Kielty to go back to the fence in front of the Boston bullpen, literally bend over backwards, reach in, and rob Nixon of a home run—that would have complemented a day where he also hit a single and a triple.

"It was one of the best catches I've ever seen here," said Nixon, who, over the course of his Boston career, lost a few homers to catches like Kielty's.

To balance the books, Kielty took a home run away from Casey Kotchman of the Angels on a similar play in the first inning of the first game he played for the Sox, on August 19, 2007, at Fenway. Kielty also had two hits in that game, but in hitting the wall to rob Kotchman, Kielty suffered a rib injury that bothered him for the rest of the season.

* * *

Red Sox players have made other memorable catches—memorable especially in the era of film and videotape—in places other than Fenway Park. Carl Yastrzemski's over-the-shoulder catch of Tom Tresh's line drive in the ninth inning of Billy Rohr's almost no-hitter at Yankee Stadium on April 6, 1967, set the tone for an entire season, as Ken Coleman described:

"Yastrzemski is going hard, way back, way back...and he dives...and makes a TREMENDOUS catch...One of the greatest catches we've ever seen by Yastrzemski in left field."

Center fielder Reggie Smith raced back to the nine-foot-high wall at RFK Stadium, climbed it on a dead run, and went three feet higher to rob Frank Howard of the Senators during the 1969 season, a catch that Dick Williams said was, "The greatest catch I ever saw in all my years as a player, coach, and manager."

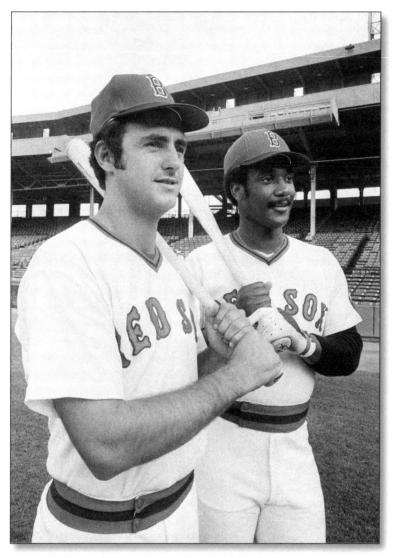

Boston Red Sox rookie sensations Fred Lynn, left, and Jim Rice, in Boston, on August 4, 1975. Both outfielders possess exceptional hitting ability. Boston manager Darrell Johnson said, "You can't say enough about those two young men." (AP PHOTO)

And on July 27, 1975, Fred Lynn made a sliding catch in left-center as left fielder Jim Rice leapt over him to help Bill Lee beat the Yankees 1–0 in the first game of what became a doubleheader sweep at Shea Stadium.

Evans, Brunansky, Zupcic, even Hooper—great catches all of them, and among the best ever at Fenway Park, but the title of No. 1 catch of all time there still has to go to Al Luplow.

CHAPTER 19

GREATEST QUOTES

The Boston Red Sox have been among the most heavily covered teams in professional sports essentially since 1901, their first year in the American League, and even through the dark days of the 1920s. Red Sox players, managers, and executives have said many memorable things through those years, and here is a sampling of some of the best.

> "There have been no ultimations."
> —Red Sox manager John McNamara
> on June 16, 1988, in Baltimore.

McNamara had called a press conference to say he would not answer any more questions about his job status. In the aftermath of Boston's stunning World Series loss to the Mets in 1986, the Red Sox had a terrible '87 season. General manager Lou Gorman shored up the Boston bullpen by acquiring Lee Smith in the off-season and expectations were high for 1988. However, the Red Sox got off to a mediocre start and in mid-June found themselves in fifth place playing just .500 ball at 30–30.

The calls for McNamara's firing got louder by the day, and when his team arrived in Baltimore on June 16 to begin a four-game series, McNamara summoned the traveling press corps to a surprise news conference in the tiny visiting manager's office under the stands.

McNamara hated the press, so everyone there figured something big was going on. There was not. McNamara, not especially articulate, opened the press conference with the "ultimations" statement and followed up by saying he would no longer answer questions regarding his job status. There were not that many more questions to answer, anyway. Just a little less than a month later, with Boston just one game above .500, McNamara was fired.

> "It really closes the coffin on a great career."
> —Roger Clemens on July 24, 1989,
> in Cooperstown, New York.

The Rocket Man was asked about Carl Yastrzemski's pending induction into the Baseball Hall of Fame. Clemens and the Red Sox were at Cooperstown for the annual Hall of Fame game, an event that has since been discontinued. That Clemens was at the event was to his credit. Sox reliever Lee Smith was a no-show and didn't bother explaining why—he just accepted the fine and took the day off.

The Hall of Fame game reached a point where teams were using public relations personnel, minor leaguers, and coaches to put enough players on the Doubleday Field diamond.

> "Any manager who can't get along with a .400 hitter is crazy."
> —Red Sox manager Joe McCarthy in Sarasota, Florida,
> at the opening of spring training in 1948.

In '48, McCarthy was the first new Red Sox manager since Joe Cronin was hired in 1935. McCarthy had managed the Yankees to eight pennants in 15 full seasons before being hired by Boston. In New York he developed a reputation as a no-nonsense boss with a pretty strict set of rules that included a dress code requiring his players to wear neckties whenever out in public.

Sox left fielder Ted Williams did not wear neckties, so the baseball world was anxious to see how McCarthy would react when Williams came down to breakfast at the team hotel on the first official day of spring training in 1948. Williams arrived tieless and McCarthy subsequently explained why he allowed it.

> "Cory Bailey wasn't wearing a (foolish) dress. It was a
> jumper, with a nice, blousy shirt and cowboy boots."
> —BOSTON MANAGER BUTCH HOBSON
> IN TORONTO ON SEPTEMBER 21, 1993.

The Sox, long out of contention in the AL East race, arrived in Toronto for the final stop on their last road trip of the season. Tradtionally, the last road trip included rookie hazing and in '93 that involved having the rookies dress up like women. So dress up they did, and the team left Yankee Stadium for Toronto on the night of September 19.

Reporters covering the team wrote about the hazing. When team president John Harrington read about it he was furious, and he called Hobson to tell him that you just can't have Boston Red Sox players traipsing through LaGuardia Airport in dresses.

Hobson had assumed that nobody would write about the hazing. September 20 was a day off, so he had a day to stew about it, and when the visiting clubhouse at the SkyDome opened up on the afternoon of September 21, the manager called in the press corps and opened verbal fire.

Hobson was livid. He could not understand how anyone could have written about the hazing, and he was in deep doo-doo with Harrington because of it, and even worse than that, the reporting was inaccurate. Hobson said he was smart enough to not let reliever Ken Ryan walk around in a short skirt, not with, "Them hairy legs of his." And as for Cory Bailey? The right-handed setup man was not, as reported, wearing a (foolish) dress. Hobson then described the outfit as if the fact that it was a jumper and not a dress made much of a difference.

> "That's not the story of this game. When I got here,
> I thought that Hillegas was a left-hander, so I put

Cerone in there. When I found out Hillegas was a righty, I could have changed it, but I said screw it—I penciled (Cerone) in and I'll leave him there. It turned out to be a good gaffe."

—Red Sox manager Joe Morgan on May 3, 1989,
at the original Comiskey Park in Chicago.

Morgan opened up his postgame press conference after Boston beat the White Sox 8–4 at the original Comiskey Park by admitting that he had confused Shawn Hillegas with Paul Kilgus, a southpaw on the White Sox pitching staff.

Cerone wound up going 1-for-3 with three RBI. He hit a two-run homer in the top of the sixth to snap a 3–3 tie and in the eighth drove home Nick Esasky with a safety squeeze bunt. Typical of the way things happened for Morgan was that the victory moved Boston into first place in the AL East.

The next day, White Sox manager Jeff Torborg was asked if he would have admitted to not knowing which hand the opposition pitcher threw with and replied, "I wouldn't have even told my wife."

"Just throw it down the middle. That's the best they can do."

—Boston catcher John Flaherty to pitcher
Scott Taylor during a mound conference
at Fenway Park on September 23, 1992.

Taylor, a southpaw, was making his first—it turned out to be his only—major league start against the Indians on a cold September night with the wind blowing in directly from left field. In the first inning, Cleveland's Carlos Baerga's shot to left was knocked down by the wind for an out. In the third, Glenallen Hill connected on a fly ball to center that was snuffed out by the wind.

In the top of the fourth, Taylor was nibbling and got behind in the count to Indians shortstop Felix Fermin and Flaherty went to the mound to remind his pitcher of what the wind had done to the two fly balls earlier. Taylor took Flaherty's advice and, in turn, Fermin smashed a line drive off the wall but was thrown out at second trying for two; Baerga doubled off the wall; Albert Belle hit one over the wall for a two-run homer; Carlos Martinez flied to right; Reggie Jefferson tripled to center; Mark Whiten walked; and Hill hit a three-run homer.

With the Indians ahead 5–0, Taylor was relieved by Paul Quantrill. Although Taylor spent part of 1993 with the Red Sox as a reliever, the September 23 game was his only start with Boston, or any other big league team.

"No. I got Martinez to swing at the illusion of strike three."
—RED SOX RELIEVER ROB MURPHY ON
JULY 31, 1990, AT FENWAY PARK.

Murphy struck out White Sox third baseman Carlos Martinez to end a 7–2 Boston victory at Fenway Park on July 31, 1990. With the count 3–2 and two men on base with two out, Murphy threw a changeup that was way high and outside that Martinez swung at and missed to end the game. A reporter suggested that Murphy caught a break by getting Martinez to swing at ball four.

Murphy was in a sense one of those stereotypical eccentric southpaws, except that he was enormously intelligent and looked at baseball as a stopover on the way to the rest of his life, not the culmination of it.

Later that season, on August 15 in Oakland, Murphy was brought in to replace Daryl Irvine in a 2–2 game in the bottom of the tenth with the bases loaded, one out, and Mark McGwire up. McGwire hit a grand slam off the Budweiser sign on the facing of the second deck to deliver a 6–2 Athletics victory.

"I could have walked him, but it would have taken longer," Murphy said after that game.

"He is one for his last one."
—A PRESS RELEASE FROM THE RED SOX PUBLIC RELATIONS
DEPARTMENT REGARDING THE SIGNING OF VETERAN FREE AGENT
OUTFIELDER BERNARD GILKEY ON JULY 4, 2000,
AFTER HE WAS RELEASED BY THE DIAMONDBACKS.

What the press release failed to mention was that, while Gilkey had a hit in his last at-bat in an Arizona uniform, he went 0-for-28 and 1-for-47 prior to that hit, a single that lifted his average from .097 to .110.

Gilkey went 3-for-4 with a single, double, home run, and four RBIs in his debut game for Boston on July 4 at Minnesota, but finished the year with a .231 average for the Sox.

"I'm not sure if we'll look in-house, or out-house."
—RED SOX GENERAL MANAGER LOU GORMAN
IN THE WINTER OF 1992-93.

Gorman was answering questions about to how the Sox were going to go about hiring a new general manager. At the end of the 1993 season, Gorman was moved to an advisory position after 10 years as general manager. Boston wound up looking out-house as it brought down Massachusetts native Dan Duquette from Montreal. His reign as GM lasted until the John Henry group bought the franchise in the spring of 2002.

"Why don't you try on Kenny's dress?"
—RED SOX CATCHER TONY PENA
ON THE NIGHT OF SEPTEMBER 19, 1993.

The Sox were traveling to Toronto for the final road series of the season and it was the rookie hazing trip. Boston's veterans had forced the rookies to dress in women's clothing and pitcher Cory Bailey was having trouble fitting into his outfit. Pena suggested he wear what reliever Ken Ryan was going to put on.

The incident nearly got manager Butch Hobson fired when team president John Harrington read about it in the papers the next morning.

> "We're a bunch of idiots, but we're grownup idiots now."
>
> —JOHNNY DAMON AT TROPICANA FIELD
> IN ST. PETERSBURG ON SEPTEMBER 28, 2004.

The 2004 Red Sox were baseball's version of The Wild Bunch, and Damon and Kevin Millar were the ringleaders. The year before, Millar had invented the rallying cry "Cowboy Up." It got the Sox to the seventh game of the ALCS but didn't get them all the way to the World Series.

The '04 Red Sox clinched a Wild Card playoff berth on the night of September 27 by beating the Tampa Bay Devil Rays 7–3 at Tropicana Field. The on-field celebration and clubhouse festivities were relatively subdued in relation to the wild scene at Fenway Park in September of 2003 when Boston clinched a Wild Card berth there. Damon was asked about the difference in the celebrations, and his response created the "Idiots" persona that characterized the Red Sox's wild ride through the 2004 playoffs.

> "The sun will rise, the sun will set, and I'll have lunch."
>
> —RED SOX GENERAL MANAGER LOU GORMAN
> IN WINTER HAVEN, FLORIDA, ON MARCH 7, 1987.

Incumbent Cy Young Award winner Roger Clemens had just walked out of spring training in a contract dispute and Gorman was asked what he was going to do as a result. Clemens was gone from camp for 29 days. After missing most of spring training, Clemens went 20–9 with 18 complete games during the regular season and won his second straight Cy Young Award.

> "You have to watch out for those reporters. They ask you questions, they write down your answers, and then they put 'em in the paper."
> —RED SOX PITCHING COACH BILL FISCHER, GIVING ADVICE TO ROOKIES ON WHAT TO EXPECT FROM THE MEDIA.

> "What can I say—just tip my hat and call the Yankees my daddy. I can't find a way to beat them at this point."
> —PEDRO MARTINEZ AFTER BEING BEATEN BY NEW YORK AT FENWAY PARK ON SEPTEMBER 24, 2004.

During his years in Boston, Martinez was the best starting pitcher in baseball, but by 2004 he had started to wear out. While Martinez had a well-deserved reputation for being a bit self-possessed and prima-donnaish, he was extremely intelligent, sensitive, clever, insightful, and generally an excellent interview. Over the years he had pitched several memorable games against the Yankees including a 17-strikeout one-hitter in the Bronx on September 10, 1999, but as time passed New York treated him the way the Red Sox treated Mariano Rivera—like just another pitcher.

On September 19, 2004, Martinez faced New York in Yankee Stadium and was charged with eight runs in five innings in a blowout loss. He sought redemption for that in his next start, also against the

Red Sox manager Terry Francona takes the ball from pitcher Pedro Martinez in the sixth innning of the Red Sox game against the New York Yankees on Sunday, September 19, 2004, at New York's Yankee Stadium. Martinez allowed eight runs on eight hits in five innings. (AP Photo/Kathy Willens)

Yankees, but at Fenway Park. Martinez pitched well, and going into the top of the eighth he had a 4–3 lead. In a span of four batters, he gave up a home run to Hideki Matsui, a double to Bernie Williams, struck out Jorge Posada, and allowed a Ruben Sierra single to drive in the go-ahead run.

After the game, in a tiny interview room under the first-base grandstand at Fenway, Martinez opened up about his frustrations to a crowd of reporters and radio and TV broadcasters. During the ALCS games at Yankee Stadium, Martinez was serenaded by loud chants of "Who's Your Daddy?" He pitched poorly there in two appearances, but had the ultimate satisfaction of winning Game 3 of the World Series and of being there when his team won Game 7.

> "I'm a flag-waving, gun-carrying, four-wheel-drive kind of a guy—and so's my wife."
> —MIKE GREENWELL AT FORT MYERS
> DURING SPRING TRAINING, 1996.

Greenwell was never at a loss for words, even when he technically wasn't talking to reporters. He was from the Fort Myers area originally, immensely proud of being from the south and never missed a chance to remind those who engaged him in conversation of his heritage. This conversation simply took an unexpected grammatical turn at the end.

> "It makes me very erotic."
> —ROGER CLEMENS ON JUNE 16, 1989,
> AT CHICAGO'S ORIGINAL COMISKEY PARK.

Clemens had shut out the White Sox 2–0 striking out 12 and giving up just two hits. He pitched the game on five days' rest instead of his usual four and was asked how working on extra rest usually affected him. Clemens was a walking malaprop at times. For instance, he often said that things had been, "Taken out of content."

172

DAISUKE MATSUZAKA

He was such a major addition to the family that the Red Sox actually had to remodel the house when they brought Daisuke Matsuzaka to Boston for the 2007 season.

The Matsuzaka signing was so much of a big deal in his native Japan that the Sox had to renovate the Fenway Park press box to take care of the crush of reporters expected to follow him on a daily basis once he arrived. They had to hire translators, too, and for the heck of it, brought along a Japanese relief pitcher to keep him company, Hideki Okajima, a move that turned out far better than they had ever hoped.

Boston's previous forays into Asia to pick up talent had not worked especially well. Native South Korean Jin-Ho Cho made his debut in 1998 and Japanese product Tomo Ohka in 1999. Neither made an impact with Boston, although Ohka pitched in the majors into 2007. More significant stories were the two fights they had while teammates on the Pawtucket Red Sox.

For the 2001 season, the Sox signed veteran Hideo Nomo who, like Matsuzaka, had had a legendary career in Japan and who came over to join the Dodgers in 1995 and was named National League Rookie of the Year. Nomo pitched a no-hitter in Baltimore in his first Red Sox start, and a one-hitter against the Blue Jays seven weeks later, becoming the first Boston pitcher since Howard Ehmke in 1923 to have a no-hitter and one-hitter in the same season. Otherwise, Nomo was good, not great, and finished with a 13–10 record. Ominously, Nomo had a problem with walks—96 of them in 198 innings—and that was an issue for Matsuzaka later, as well.

Asian pitchers Sang-Hoon Lee, Sun-Woo Kim, and B.K. Kim were all tried and found wanting. B.K. Kim arrived from the Diamondbacks in a trade for Shea Hillenbrand and Boston had high hopes for him, but B.K. Kim was an oddball who once fell asleep in the owner's box at City of Palms Park in Fort Myers, got locked in, and had to be rescued, and who gave Fenway fans the finger when he was booed during the introduction for the 2003 playoffs.

One of the heroes of the 2004 World Series victory was born in Okinawa, Dave Roberts, but Roberts grew up in the United States and went to college at UCLA.

Matsuzaka had been the best pitcher in Japan's Pacific League for seven years when he helped his country win the inaugural World Baseball Classic in 2006, winning all three of his starts and compiling a 1.38 ERA. After that season his Pacific League team, the Seibu Lions, put the rights to sign him up for silent auction, with Boston's bid of $51.1 million carrying the day. Having won those rights, the Sox finally agreed on a deal with him for $52 million over six years.

Matsuzaka made his debut in a Boston uniform on a cold day in Kansas City, April 5, 2007. He was excellent in beating the Royals 4–1, allowing just one run in seven innings while striking out 10.

Through May 25, Matsuzaka was 7–2 and looked to be worth the money the Sox spent on him. On May 30, though, he gave up 12 hits in $5\frac{2}{3}$ innings in a loss to the Indians. He lost to Oakland on June 5, throwing 130 pitches in seven innings then lost his next start as well.

A pattern had emerged with Matsuzaka—he was falling behind hitters, often recovering to get outs, but issuing too many walks and exiting games early, putting a strain on the Boston bullpen. In three starts from June 10–22 he walked 12. In three starts from July 14–24, he walked 11, as he also did in three starts from August 10–22 and September 8–22.

As the season progressed, Matsuzaka regressed. In his final eight starts he was just 2–4 with a 7.14 ERA and finished the year with an okay, but not thrilling, record of 15–12. When Matsuzaka started the year, there was some question about the legitimacy of his Rookie of the Year credentials given his eight years in Japan, but when it came time for the voting, he was never really a serious candidate and teammate Dustin Pedroia won the balloting.

Matsuzaka's record was better in the postseason, but in four starts, he never went more than $5\frac{1}{3}$ innings. His biggest moment in a Red Sox uniform happened in Game 3 of the World Series in Colorado, when he was the winning pitcher in Boston's 10–5 victory and drove in two runs with a single to left in the third inning.

As Matsuzaka bumped along through his first season, the Sox were quick to caution that there was an inevitable adjustment period for a player coming over from Japan, even though that had not happened in the case of Seattle's Ichiro Suzuki, and

Boston Red Sox starting pitcher Daisuke Matsuzaka delivers against the Oakland Athletics during the first inning of a baseball game at Fenway Park in Boston, on Sunday, August 3, 2008. (AP Photo/Winslow Townson)

did not happen in the case of Okajima, who had developed into one of the league's best setup relievers. In any case, Matsuzaka was expected to show substantial improvement in his second season, and he did.

He went from 15–12 with a 4.40 ERA to 18–3 with a stingy 2.90 ERA. In terms of winning percentage, it was one of the best seasons ever by a Boston starter. In 2008, with Josh Beckett injured, Matsuzaka was the Red Sox's Opening Day starter in the Tokyo Dome. He spent time on the disabled list with some minor shoulder soreness and wound up making three fewer starts and pitching 37 fewer innings than in '07.

His control problems continued—94 walks in 167⅔ innings—but he managed to win, sometimes in curious fashion. He won five games in which he pitched the minimum five innings. He won a game in Detroit on May 5 in which he walked eight and struck out just one. He won two games in which he walked six. Matsuzaka was a master at loading up the bases, then leaving everyone stranded, which begged the question—if he is good enough to get everybody out with the bases loaded, why can't he keep them from getting loaded in the first place?

As the season wore on, Matsuzaka began to pitch more efficiently and had games in which he left the other team looking overmatched. His combined record for two seasons was 33–15. It had taken a while, but it finally looked as though Dice-K was proving to be worth the more than $100 million the Sox invested in him.

CHAPTER 20

MANNY BEING MANNY

Manny Ramirez spent almost eight full, tumultuous seasons in a Red Sox uniform, during which Boston won 706 games in the regular season and lost 536, won 28 postseason games and lost 15, and played in two World Series and won them both.

Ramirez hit 274 home runs, drove in 868 runs, and batted .312 in a Red Sox uniform. It was a great career, and a stop on the way to the Baseball Hall of Fame, but his behavior was so outrageous at times that it led to a new phrase entering the unofficial Red Sox dictionary—Manny being Manny.

Ramirez rarely spoke to members of the news media, and when he did what he said often did not make a lot of sense. That was not the case all the time, though. Occasionally he would be entirely reasonable, rational, and conversational, which not only added to the whole "Manny being Manny" persona, but led to questions about just how real it was.

Part of it might have been an act to avoid having to explain the whys and hows of what he did, but I had a chance one summer day to watch Ramirez completely away from baseball, and that unguarded Manny was very much the same one who did unexplainable things on the baseball field.

The Red Sox had a day off on Thursday, June 1, 2006. They were in the midst of a three-city road trip that started in Toronto and ended in New York. The night before they had beaten the Blue Jays, 8–6. Boston's next game was scheduled for Friday in Detroit.

Manny Ramirez hits a three-run home run in the sixth inning against the Oakland Athletics in Game 5 of the American League Division Series playoff game on Monday, October 6, 2003, in Oakland, California.
(AP Photo/Ben Margot)

While the team flies from city to city on a charter, players can make their own travel arrangements if they wish, for instance, to do something like spend an extra day and night in Toronto as opposed to Detroit—and that is exactly what Ramirez did on that trip.

At the time, Toronto's Lester B. Pearson Airport was under construction and commuter flights to places like Detroit left from satellite gates at the far reaches of the field. To get there, fliers had to take buses and then wait for their flights in cramped, temporary quarters. I had arrived in plenty of time for my flight to Detroit that morning and had plugged in my laptop to get some work done, when down the hallway, a bag of suits slung over his shoulder, came Ramirez. Alongside him was Ino Guerrero, who was listed in the Red Sox media guide as Major League Staff Assistant and who pitched some batting practice, but was in fact employed as Ramirez' personal assistant.

Smiling, Ramirez ambled up to the gate agent and amiably told her, "I lost my ticket."

That was utterly impossible, she said. Nobody can get to this point in the airport if they've lost their ticket, especially if they were flying out of the country. It would be a security breach. Something would have had to have gone dreadfully wrong for a person to be able to stroll to the deepest reaches of the airport having lost his or her ticket.

So, she said, you must mean you've lost your boarding pass.

"Uh-uh," Ramirez countered. "I lost my ticket."

The gate agent was just about to sound the alarm and clear the whole area when Guerrero walked up to her and said, "He's lost this," pulling a boarding pass from his shirt pocket. With a huge sigh of relief, the gate agent told Ramirez that kind of thing happens all the time, we can just print you out another boarding pass, and here you go. Crisis solved; life returns to normal in that corner of Canada.

The plane to Detroit was a small one, and the gate was at the end of a hallway, so there was not a lot of foot traffic. Ramirez and Guerrero sat silently next to each other and Ramirez was mostly left alone with his thoughts, whatever they might have been. He is pretty distinctive looking, however, and any passing sports fan would recognize him—which eventually happened.

When it did, Ramirez acted graciously, greeting the fan with a nod and a smile and signing whatever was given to him. Finally, it was time to board the little plane for Detroit and through the gate went the 20 or so passengers bound for Michigan. The plane had little room for carry-on luggage, so we had to leave most of our things out on the runway to be gate-checked, a process that went without a hitch and we were soon in the air.

Upon landing, we were instructed to stay behind the yellow line and wait for our baggage to be brought over after we deplaned—which all but one of us did. Ramirez, seeing his bag sitting in the luggage compartment at the rear of the plane, casually strolled across the runway to get it.

More yelling and panic. Security! Security! Sir, you can't go there. Hearing the commotion, Ramirez stopped and looked around. A baggage handler walked over to him, took him by the arm, led him back behind the yellow line, and things returned to normal. We all had our bags brought over to us, and Ramirez and Guerrero headed inside the airport.

There was a long passageway from our landing gate to the airport exit and Ramirez, suit bag slung over his shoulder, walked along next to Guerrero, who had a bag on his shoulder and was pulling a small suitcase. Suddenly, Ramirez took the suit bag off his shoulder and put it on Guerrero's empty one, and off they went for the Sox's hotel in suburban Detroit.

It was Manny being Manny, but with nobody looking, or at least with nobody watching on TV, and in a relatively private setting. That was Ramirez, Mr. Magoo in a Red Sox cap, blithely strolling through life while the Ino Guerreros of the world straightened out the turmoil left behind.

* * *

For most of his stay in Boston, Ramirez's eccentricities were tolerated by his teammates, if not his bosses, and looked on good-naturedly. Some of them were quite harmless, like his occasional trips into the bottom of the Green Monster to do who knows what—it wasn't to answer the call of nature, since there are no toilets in the base of the wall. Or, like the time on July 21, 2004, when he stepped in front of center fielder Johnny Damon's throw and acted as a cutoff man about 20 feet from where Damon was standing; Baltimore's David Newhan turned the play into an inside-the-park home run.

Ramirez habitually reported to spring training after everyone else, although never so late that it was a violation of the game's Collective Bargaining Agreement. He had various relatives who got sick and needed his attention. He didn't join the rest of the 2007 World Series champions when they were honored at a White House reception.

In 2002, when he was on a rehab assignment in Pawtucket, he lost a diamond earring at McCoy Stadium running the bases. In Baltimore on May 14, 2008, he made a great catch against the left-field fence then climbed halfway up it to high-five a fan.

But Ramirez also did things that were not so innocent and endearing. During the last week of August 2003, he came down with pharyngitis—Pedro Martinez had it, too, so it seemed to be going around—and could not play in a series against the Yankees at Fenway Park, but was seen out dining with pal Enrique Wilson, a New York infielder.

On September 9, 2002, late in Grady Little's first year as manager, Ramirez hit a hard ground ball back to the mound in the third inning of a game at Tampa Bay. Instead of running to first, Ramirez turned directly around and headed for the dugout, and in effect was thrown out by 95 feet by Devil Rays pitcher Tanyon Sturtze.

Little left Ramirez in the game and in the seventh, he hit a home run to break a 3–3 tie as Boston went on to win, 6–3. The next day, Little told reporters before the game that he had made a mistake by not pulling Ramirez from the game the night before when he didn't run out the ground ball.

On September 1, 2003, Ramirez refused to enter a game in Philadelphia as a pinch-hitter; Trot Nixon's grand slam in the ninth inning won it for the Sox. On July 6, 2008, Ramirez was sent up to pinch-hit by Terry Francona in the ninth inning of a 4–4 game at Yankee Stadium. Facing Mariano Rivera, Ramirez's bat never left his shoulder as he took three straight called strikes.

By 2008, the teammates who had given Ramirez so much leeway through the years had grown tired of him. Previously, they figured they were better off with him than without him. In July '08, with the distracting Ramirez trying to force a trade, Francona and most of the players in uniform wanted him gone and Theo Epstein acquiesced.

Manny being Manny meant Manny being gone. Was it all an act, or was Ramirez really not much more than a nine-year-old with a major-league bat? As his finals days in a Boston uniform showed, Ramirez was capable of doing what he had to do to get his way, but as most of the rest of his Sox career demonstrated, he was simply a gifted athlete who had never been forced to grow up.

DUTCH THE CLUTCH

As good as Ted Williams and Dom DiMaggio were in left field and center field for the Red Sox, the team could never really find a right fielder to match. They tried Lou Finney, Catfish Metkovich, Sam Mele, and Al Zarilla, but for the Williams-era Sox, there was usually an open tryout going on for right field—that's how Clyde Vollmer came to be Boston's right fielder on July 1, 1951.

Vollmer had arrived in town by way of the Washington Senators, whom the Red Sox traded with on May 8, 1950. Boston sent outfielder Tommy O'Brien, who was at the end of the line, and third baseman Merl Combs, who never really got in line, to the Senators in exchange for Vollmer.

After a very promising beginning—on May 31, 1942, playing for the Reds, Vollmer hit the first pitch he ever saw in the majors for a home run—things slowed down. Vollmer followed up that first-pitch home run by going 3-for-42 then his career was derailed by three years in the army. He was a native Cincinnatian and was a high school star at Western Hills, where Pete Rose later played, a school that eventually sent Russ Nixon, Tommy Helms, Tuffy Rhodes, and Don Zimmer to the Red Sox.

Vollmer was a spare outfielder with nothing to suggest he would ever be more than that until July 1951, when he went on a hitting spree that would become the gold standard for Red Sox hot streaks and earn him the nickname, "Dutch the Clutch."

At the end of June, Vollmer had only 76 at-bats and had posted a .263 average with three home runs and 12 RBIs. Only the 4th of July, the Red Sox played a holiday doubleheader in Philadelphia against the Athletics and Vollmer went 2-for-8 on the day; his second hit was a solo home run in the ninth inning of Boston's 9–5 victory in the second game.

That kept him in the lineup, and on July 7 at Fenway Park with the Yankees in town, Vollmer hit a grand slam off Allie Reynolds in the bottom of the first inning to propel the Red Sox to a 10–4 victory. The next game was also versus New York at Fenway and Vollmer homered again, this time hitting a two-run shot off Vic Raschi in the sixth inning to help Boston gain a 6–3 victory over the eventual American League pennant winners.

Vollmer had, in a span of five games and 18 at-bats, hit as many home runs as he had hit in his previous 76 at-bats. After the game of July 8, it was time for the All-Star break, but that did nothing to cool off Vollmer, who hit another home run in the first game of a doubleheader at Comiskey Park in Chicago on July 12 to extend his streak to three straight games with a homer.

The White Sox blanked Vollmer in the second game of the doubleheader, but he struck again the next day with a solo home run off Chicago southpaw Billy Pierce in a 5–4 loss. The Red Sox and Vollmer were halfway through the month of July and he already had twice as many home runs as he had hit in April, May, and June combined—and he was just getting started.

On the 18th, with Boston at Cleveland Stadium, Vollmer's solo home run in the fifth inning off Bob Lemon was the difference in the Red Sox's 4–3 victory there. On the 19th, Vollmer hit two home runs off the Indians' Early Wynn, a two-run homer in the second inning, and a solo homer in the top of the eleventh to give the Sox a temporary 4–3 lead in a game that Cleveland came back to win, 5–4.

Boston played the Tigers in Detroit on July 21. The Sox won 6–3 thanks to Vollmer's 3-for-4 performance that included a double, a single, and a three-run home run off Virgil Trucks in the second inning. That made it four home runs in his last three games for Vollmer; in those three games he had gone 6-for-11 with five runs scored, eight RBIs, and five extra-base hits.

There was more to come.

The Red Sox returned to Fenway Park and on July 28, Vollmer became only the fourth player in franchise history to hit three home runs in a game, joining Jim Tabor, Ted Williams, and Bobby Doerr on the list. Vollmer's homer hat trick came in a 13–10 victory over the White Sox and he almost homered for the cycle. Vollmer hit a two-run shot in the first, a solo drive in the fifth, and three-run home run in the sixth, driving in six runs with a 3-for-4 performance.

He went a routine 1-for-4 the next day with a single, then finished his amazing month with a dramatic bang, etching his name in the record books in the process. The Red Sox were playing the Indians at Fenway Park on the 28th and went into the sixteenth inning with the game tied, 4–4. When Vollmer came up to bat in the last of the sixteenth, he had already singled and doubled in six previous at-bats and had driven in one of the four Boston runs.

Cleveland had Bob Feller on the mound and the Sox had the bases loaded. Vollmer unloaded them with a game-ending grand slam, the latest-in-the-game one ever hit, and with a final score of 8–4 Boston had a victory.

That was the end of Vollmer's home run orgy, but not quite the end of the month, or of his offensive surge. On July 31, he went 1-for-3 with a double and two RBIs, after which August arrived and he cooled off, although he remained a dangerous hitter. Vollmer finished with 22 homers and 85 RBIs, both second on the team to Ted Williams.

For the outstanding month of July 1951, Vollmer, a career .251 hitter, batted .314 with a slugging percentage of .725. He hit 13 homers in 26 games and just 56 home runs in 659 games for the rest of his career. He also had 40 RBIs in 26 games and managed 299 in his other 659 games.

Only two Red Sox players have ever driven in 40 runs in a month—Vollmer and Williams, who did it twice. Williams' 41 in May 1942 is the club record. At the time, Vollmer's 13 home runs in a month tied the team record set by Jimmie Foxx in August 1940 and since broken by Jackie Jensen and David Ortiz, who both had 14-homer months.

What is perhaps most amazing when one looks back at Vollmer's remarkable month of July 1951, is the company he kept in the process of hitting all of the homers and driving in all the runs. He hit home runs off Hall of Fame pitchers like Lemon, Wynn, and Feller. He is mentioned on the Sox's various home run and RBI lists with batters like Williams, Foxx, Carl Yastrzemski, and Bobby Doerr—all members of the Hall of Fame; Jensen, Fred Lynn, Mo Vaughn, and Jim Rice, all of whom were American League MVPs; Nomar Garciaparra, Manny Ramirez, and David Ortiz.

In 1952, Vollmer hit 11 home runs, two fewer than in July of '51, and had 50 RBIs. He hit .262. He played one game for Boston in 1953 before being sold back to the Senators and played the 1954 season, his final one in the major leagues, in Washington. After that, Vollmer returned to his native Cincinnati and settled into everyday life as the owner of the Lark Lounge.

It was 11 years, almost to the day, before the next Vollmer came along.

* * *

For the first part of his career, Lu Clinton was a Boston outfielder known mostly for a bizarre play in Cleveland on August 9, 1960, when a ball hit by Indians first baseman Vic Power bounced off of the right-field fence, hit Clinton in the foot, and bounced back over the stands for a home run. Until June 28, 1962, nothing had happened to overshadow that moment.

The '62 season was again shaping up to be a disappointing one in Boston. The 1961 season had featured rookies Carl Yastrzemski, Chuck Schilling, and Don Schwall, who was the American League Rookie of the Year, and it seemed as though the team was finally ready to contend again. But, as June drew to a close, the Red Sox were seven games under .500 and in ninth place.

For his part, Clinton was the lousiest player on a lousy team. Through June 28 he was hitting exactly .100, having gone for 6-for-60 with one home run and seven RBIs. On June 29, manager Mike Higgins put Clinton in the starting lineup for a game against the Kansas City Athletics at Fenway Park. Boston had a 2–1 lead when Clinton, batting seventh, came up in the sixth. He hit a grand slam to give the Sox a 6–1 lead, then belted a two-run homer in the eighth and made it 9–3.

That was only the beginning. Clinton stayed in the lineup, played right field, and batted mostly seventh. Over a 19-game stretch that began on June 28, he put together perhaps the hottest long-term batting streak the Red Sox had ever seen, or would ever see.

Here are the highlights.

In a July 4 doubleheader at Fenway versus the Twins, Clinton went 7-for-8 with two doubles and two home runs. He missed hitting for the cycle by one hit, a triple, in both games. In the second game, his two-run homer in the second gave the Sox a 2–1 lead; he singled and scored in the fourth to make it 4–1; he had an RBI double in the fifth to make it 5–1; and he singled and scored in the seventh to make it 8–5. Clinton was 12-for-15 in a four-game series with Minnesota that concluded with that doubleheader.

On July 7 in Los Angeles against the Angels, Clinton's three-run homer in the fourth was the key hit in a 5–4 Boston victory.

On July 12, in the second game of a doubleheader at Kansas City, Clinton homered in the second to make it 1–0, homered in the fifth to make it 2–1, and hit a two-run triple in the top of the eleventh to give the Sox a 7–4 lead in a game they eventually won, 9–4.

The next night, Clinton hit for the cycle as Boston won 11–10 in 15 innings. His single in the top of the fifteenth drove in what proved to be the winning run. He was 5-for-7 with a walk, four runs scored, and four RBIs.

On July 20, his bases-loaded triple in the first inning was the key hit in Boston's 8–4 victory over the White Sox at Fenway Park. And that was it, although it was more than enough.

Clinton went 0-for-4 the next night and was 5-for-36 over the next 10 games. He finished the season batting .294 with 18 homers and 75 RBIs. Clinton hit 22 homers in 1963, but batted just .232. He was traded to the Angels for Lee Thomas in 1964 and bounced around the American League for a couple of more years.

He finished his career with the Yankees in 1967, just as the Red Sox were rewriting their franchise history. Clinton settled in Wichita, Kansas, where he ran a heating oil business and died young in 1997. He was just 60 years old.

Clinton's memorable streak lasted for 19 games, during which he went 38-for-76 (.500), scored 25 runs, and drove in 29. Clinton had seven doubles, four triples, and nine home runs. His slugging percentage was 1.053, his on-base average .537. During the peak of the streak, nine games starting on July 3, he was 24-for-41 (.585).

* * *

While Clinton was going crazy in that July, Yastrzemski was beginning to show why the Sox had thought he was a good bet to replace Ted Williams in left field. Yaz finished 1962 with a .296 average, 30 points better than his rookie year, and was just under the 20 homer 100 RBI mark. Still, Yastrzemski would not begin to establish Hall of Fame credentials until his Clintonian and Vollmerian performance in the last weeks of 1967.

The first sign that '67 would be a different kind of year for Yastrzemski happened on April 14 in Yankee Stadium, when he made a diving catch in left field of Tom Tresh's deep line drive. At the time, the play preserved Billy Rohr's no-hitter and remains one of the finest defensive plays ever made by a Boston outfielder.

As the Impossible Dream season went along, Yastrzemski was clearly a different kind of offensive player than he had been previously. He hit

Tony Conigliaro center fielder for the Boston Red Sox, stands in center field at New York's Yankee Stadium on April 15, 1964, before memorials to baseball immortals Lou Gehrig, Miller Higgins, and Babe Ruth. (AP Photo)

for more power; he hit into fewer double plays; he hit in the clutch. But into August, Tony Conigliaro had jut about matched Yaz in terms of power, production, and clutch hits. That changed on the night of August 18 at Fenway Park when Angels pitcher Jack Hamilton's fastball smashed into the left side of Conigliaro's face, ending his season.

What was most amazing about Yastrzemski's emergence as the single most important bat in the Boston lineup was how directly it correlated with Conigliaro's beaning. On the night Conigliaro was injured, Yastrzemski went 0-for-3. Over the next three games, with the Red Sox wondering how they would replace Conigliaro's production, Yastrzemski went 6-for-10 with seven runs scored, eight RBIs, and a home run in each game.

The night after the beaning, Yastrzemski went 4-for-5 and his two-run homer in the sixth put the Sox ahead of the Angels 7–6 in game they eventually won, 12–11. Two days later, Boston swept a doubleheader from California and he homered in both games; in the second game, the Sox were down 8–1 when Yastrzemski hit a three-run home run in the fifth inning to make it a more manageable 8–4, and Boston came back to win, 9–8.

On August 25 in Chicago, in the first game of a doubleheader, Yastrzemski went 3-for-3 and scored three runs in a 7–1 victory. On August 27, also in Chicago and also in the first game of a doubleheader, Yastrzemski went 2-for-3 and hit two home runs in a 4–3 victory that has come to be known as the Tartabull Game—right fielder Jose Tartabull preserved the win by throwing Ken Berry out at home for the final out in the last of the ninth.

Less than a week later, Yastrzemski did it again. Boston was playing at Yankee Stadium on August 30 and the score was 1–1 after seven. Yaz took over for George Thomas in left field in the eighth inning and the game went into extra innings still tied, 1–1. With two out in the top of the eleventh, he hit a solo home run off Al Downing and the Red Sox won, 2–1. Then, in Washington on September 5, Yastrzemski went 3-for-4 with four RBIs, including a three-run homer and a solo shot, as the Sox beat the Senators, 8–2.

After that, Yastrzemski became merely mortal for a while. He did nothing of note through September 17, but Boston continued to contend. After losing 5–2 to the Orioles at Fenway on the 17th the Red Sox were one game out of first, but with three other teams—the Tigers, White Sox, and Twins—in a pack separated by just a game.

Through September 17, Yastrzemski was a good player having a great year. In the 12 games that followed, however, he submitted his nomination papers for the Hall of Fame. Other Boston batters—including Vollmer and Clinton—were as hot as Yastrzemski was in the last 12 games of the 1967 season, but nobody was ever as hot when it meant as much.

In the season's final 12 games, Yastrzemski was 23-for-44 (.523) with four doubles, five home runs, 16 RBIs, and 14 runs scored. In the season's final two games, what amounted to sudden-death elimination games if the Sox had lost either, he was 7-for-8.

Here are some highlights from those final 12 games.

On September 18 in Detroit, he had a single, double, and home run in four trips to the plate. Yastrzemski doubled to give Boston a 1–0 lead in the first inning; the Sox trailed 5–4 with one out in the top of the ninth and he homered to make it 5–5; Dalton Jones won the game with another home run in the tenth.

On September 20 in Cleveland, Yastrzemski went 4-for-5 with a home run and two runs scored. It was a 4–4 game with two out and nobody on base in the top of the ninth when Yaz singled; he wound up scoring the game-winning run on Reggie Smith's two-out base hit.

On September 30 at Fenway, with Boston needing a victory to tie the Twins for first and avoid being eliminated from the pennant race, he went 3-for-4. In the fifth, his second single of the game was an infield hit that drove in the run that put the Sox ahead, 2–1. In the seventh, with Boston holding a precarious 3–2 lead, his three-run home run off Jim Merritt made it 6–2 and provided the winning runs as the Sox won, 6–4.

Finally, on the last day of the season, October 1, Yastrzemski went 4-for-4 with a double and two RBIs. The two RBIs were the two biggest ones of the game and came in the bottom of the sixth, driving in the runs that turned a 2–0 deficit into a 2–2 tie. Boston eventually won the game 5–3 and the American League pennant.

Starting with the game played the night after Conigliaro was beaned, Yastrzemski was 57-for-159 (.358) with 16 home runs and 40 RBIs in 45 games. Red Sox fans had seen that kind of hitting before, but only rarely, and never on such an important stage.

For Yastrzemski, it helped set the tone for his eventual trip to Cooperstown and it was a stretch of hitting the likes of which has only happened two other times in Red Sox history.

CHAPTER 22

THE GREATEST
SOX HOME RUN

The image of Carlton Fisk waving, leaping, and dancing in Fenway Park just after midnight on October 22, 1975, is one of the most remembered and replayed moments in both Red Sox and baseball history. The occasion was Fisk's twelfth-inning home run to beat the Cincinnati Reds in Game 6 of what is still considered by some the greatest game of the greatest World Series ever played. That would make that historic swing the greatest home run in Red Sox history, right?

Not quite.

Any list of the greatest Red Sox home runs ever would include Fisk's solo shot and it would have to be near the top. But right on top—no. How about in third place, behind the one Dave Henderson hit in the 1986 ALCS and the one Bernie Carbo hit four innings before Fisk in Game 6 of that '75 World Series?

Ranking home runs is never easy and entirely subjective, and the passage of time often changes the reality of the moment. When it happened, Henderson's home run in Game 6 of the 1986 World Series would probably have been at the top of the list. The events of the bottom of the tenth doomed it to a place in the footnotes of Red Sox history.

Neither Henderson's ALCS home run in 1986 nor Carbo's in '75 were what has come to be known as a walk-off home run, but that does not diminish their significance. There is no logic to the way baseball games and seasons take on lives of their own, but the fact is that they do. While Henderson's homer did not win Game 5 of the 1986 ALCS, it turned the emotional tide in Boston's favor and led to the Sox eventually winding up in the World Series. Carbo's, likewise, turned a reasonably interesting 1975 World Series into an event that has become a chapter in baseball history unto itself.

Here are the ten greatest home runs in Red Sox history.

1. October 12, 1986, Dave Henderson

Through eight innings of Game 5, it had been the worst postseason performance by any Red Sox team anywhere, any time. Boston lost three of the first four games of the ALCS to the Angels and the night before Game 5, had blown a 3–0 lead in the bottom of the ninth before losing in 11 innings. The Sox's lethargy continued in the fifth game at Anaheim Stadium and they trailed 5–2 going into the top of the ninth with the Angels and manager Gene Mauch both just three outs away from their first-ever visits to the World Series.

Mike Witt was on the mound as Bill Buckner led off the ninth and Buckner singled. Boston manager John McNamara sent Dave Stapleton in to run for Buckner—let's not get ahead of ourselves here, just leave it at that—and Jim Rice followed by taking a called third strike for the first out of the inning.

Next up was Don Baylor and he homered. It was a 5–4 game with one out and the Sox had at least two swings left—Boston's chances at extending the series had improved from hopeless to unlikely. They became even more unlikely when Witt got Dwight Evans to pop to third, then Mauch brought in lefty Gary Lucas to face lefty Rich Gedman.

Lucas hit Gedman, putting the tying run on first, even if it was the slow-footed Gedman. Mauch took out Lucas and brought in Donnie Moore to face Henderson, who had been uniformly dreadful for Boston since coming over from Seattle in an August trade. Henderson looked overmatched in the at-bat, but he was able to work the count to 2–2.

The next pitch was low and outside. A smart hitter would have reached out and gone the other way and hoped the ball found some outfield grass in right or right-center. Instead, Henderson snapped his

Dave Henderson watches the flight of his ninth-inning homer that put Boston ahead of the Angels 6–5 in Anaheim, California, on Sunday, October 12, 1986. It is the greatest home run in Red Sox history. (AP PHOTO/JIM GERBERICH)

wrists and sent the ball in the air towards left-center. At first, it looked like a routine fly ball; instead, it kept carrying and carrying and Angels left fielder Brian Downing watched it disappear over the fence.

Gedman scored ahead of Henderson, who pirouetted after he left the batter's box and realized what he had done. Red Sox 6, Angels 5. California actually tied the game in the last of the ninth and Boston didn't win it until the eleventh, when Henderson drove in the seventh run with a sacrifice fly. The Angels were cooked; Boston won the next two games, both at Fenway Park, by a combined score of 18–5, and it was on to the World Series against the Mets.

What makes Henderson's homer the greatest in Red Sox history?

No home run before or since has rescued a Boston team that was as close to extinction as Boston was in the '86 ALCS. Two outs and two strikes in the ninth—one pitch away from being embarrassed by the Angels—and Henderson's home run created the legend that 1986 became.

Years later, in an interview with ESPN.com, Henderson remembered his home run this way, "How can I not think about it? It changed my life. It turned my career around. I'm not exactly sure where it ranks among the greatest and most dramatic home runs, but I know it's right up there with Bobby Thomson, Bill Mazeroski, Carlton Fisk, Kirk Gibson, and Joe Carter. I always thought of Thomson's as the biggest or Mazeroski's and even Carter's because they won a pennant and World Series. But mine is up there."

And at the top of the list among Red Sox homers.

2. October 21, 1975, Bernie Carbo

Until the night of October 21, the 1975 World Series had been enjoyable, if not memorable. The Reds led 3–2. Game 1 and Game 5 were both lopsided, but the middle games were great ones; each was decided by one run.

Game 6, played after three days of rain at Fenway Park, wasn't much heading into the bottom of the eighth. Cincinnati had a 6–3 lead with two out, two on, and Bernie Carbo up as a pinch-hitter for pitcher

Rogelio Moret with Rawly Eastwick on the mound for the Reds. Had Carbo made an out, the '75 World Series would most likely have been filed away with the 1951 World Series, or 1943 World Series, or 1922 World Series—not really very much to remember.

Carbo came up with Fred Lynn and Rico Petrocelli on base. He never expected to hit, figuring Reds manager Sparky Anderson would replace Eastwick with a lefty after he was announced, and Sox skipper Darrell Johnson would counter with right-handed hitter Juan Beniquez. Instead, Anderson left Eastwick in, and at first it seemed like a smart move.

Carbo fell behind in the count and stayed alive by barely ticking a foul ball on a Little League swing. On the next pitch, he tied the game with a homer into the center-field bleachers. That made it 6–6; Fisk finally won it in the bottom of the twelfth.

Why was Carbo's home run even more significant than Fisk's?

Before Carbo, the '75 World Series was interesting, and a four games to two Reds victory would have been entirely predictable. In the wake of Carbo's home run, the following happened:

1. The Red Sox loaded the bases with none out in the last of the ninth and did not score thanks to George Foster's throw home from left field to nail Denny Doyle at the plate for a double play;
2. Dwight Evans made a remarkable catch in the right-field corner with one out in the top of the eleventh to take away extra bases from Joe Morgan, and a certain run from the Reds; the play became a double play when shortstop Rick Burleson beat Ken Griffey to first base;
3. Fisk's home run to lead off the bottom of the twelfth;
4. A memorable, if not as dramatic, Game 7 that saw the Reds come back from three runs down to win in the top of the ninth.

The 1975 World Series may not be the greatest one ever played, but it is a candidate. Game 6 might not be the greatest game ever played, but it is a candidate—and all because of Carbo's home run.

3. October 21, 1975, Carlton Fisk

The World Series magnifies everything, and a walk-off home run is thrilling no matter when it happens, so a World Series walk-off homer is automatically entered as historic.

Fisk would have had a Hall of Fame career even without his Game 6 home run, but the circumstances leading up to it, and the video of his reactions after the ball left his bat, have turned it into one of the most easily recognizable moments not just in Red Sox history, but all of baseball history.

4. October 17, 2004, David Ortiz

Red Sox fans had become so used to Ortiz delivering clutch hits that it almost seemed pre-ordained Boston would win Game 4 of the 2004 ALCS behind Ortiz' bat, and it did. But it took a while.

In the ninth, after Bill Mueller's single had tied the game at 4–4 and kept the Yankees from sweeping their way into the World Series, the Red Sox had runners at first and third with just one out, then the bases loaded with two out and could not score. Orlando Cabrera struck out with men at first and third. Ortiz popped to second to end the inning with the bases full.

In the top of the eleventh, Sox reliever Curtis Leskanic got Bernie Williams to fly to center with the bases loaded and two out to keep it a tie game, then Leskanic kept it 4–4 by retiring New York in the top of the twelfth despite a leadoff single by Jorge Posada.

Ex-Boston closer Tom Gordon pitched shutout ball for the Yankees in the tenth and eleventh, then Joe Torre called on workhorse Paul Quantrill for the twelfth. Quantrill broke into the majors with the Red Sox in 1992, then was traded to the Phillies in '94 for Wes Chamberlain in an awful deal.

Quantrill was looking at an inning that started with Manny Ramirez, who at that time was hitting third with Ortiz in the cleanup spot. If he got past Ramirez and Ortiz, Jason Varitek was due up third and Trot Nixon after that. The Yankees reliever had little margin for error.

Ramirez led off with a single. Ortiz followed with a walk-off home run, his second of the 2004 postseason, that carried more than 400 feet to right. Ortiz had another walk-off hit, a single, the next night and the Red Sox never stopped rolling. The game Ortiz won with his twelfth-inning homer was the first of eight in a row for Boston, the eighth victory giving the Sox their first World Series title since 1918.

5. September 18, 1967, Carl Yastrzemski

There were several times late in the season when 1967's Impossible Dream was on the verge of falling apart and September 18, with the Sox playing Detroit at Tiger Stadium, was one of those times.

Five days earlier Boston had beaten the Kansas City Athletics to finish a run where it had won four in a row and seven of eight games. The Sox were in a dead heat for first place with the Twins. Both teams were at 84–63 with the Tigers in third at 83–64.

Then, Boston went cold. The Sox lost three in a row at Fenway Park to the eighth-place Orioles. Boston headed west to begin an eight-game road trip, the first two at Detroit in a head-to-head battle with the Tigers, who had taken over first place during the Sox's slump. In a classic game, Boston went ahead 3–0 and Detroit tied it. The Sox went up 4–3 and the Tigers made it 4–4. In the bottom of the eighth, Jim Northrup's double off John Wyatt gave Detroit a 5–4 lead and the Tigers went into the ninth inning three outs away from putting Boston two games back.

It never happened.

Reliever Fred Lasher struck out Mike Andrews to start the inning, then Yastrzemski unloaded a bomb into the upper deck in right to tie it at 5–5. Ken Coleman was doing the radio play by play and his voice cracked as he hollered, "There's a drive going deep to right field...and it is TIED UP."

Mike Marshall replaced Lasher for the top of the tenth and Dalton Jones led off the inning with another shot into the second deck in right. Boston won 6–5 and instead of being two games out, had tied the Tigers for first place. The victory sent the Sox off on a four-game winning streak and the Impossible Dream was renewed and eventually fulfilled.

6. October 20, 2004, Johnny Damon

It was a game the Red Sox won 10–3, and it happened in the second inning with Boston already ahead by two runs, so at face value, Johnny Damon's grand slam in Game 7 of the 2004 ALCS seems like it should be not too much more than an interesting sidelight to a lopsided outcome. At the time, though, it seemed huge, and its value went beyond the four Red Sox runs it delivered.

Boston went into that Game 7 on the cusp of doing something no baseball team had ever done—come back and win a postseason series after trailing three games to none. David Ortiz had gotten the Red Sox off to a good start with a two-run homer in the top of the first, but this was Yankee Stadium and previous Boston teams had written an awful lot of bad history there.

Two runs seemed hardly enough.

Yankees starter Kevin Brown got Trot Nixon out to begin the second but never got another out. A single and two walks later, Brown was relieved by Javier Vazquez who came in to face Damon.

Damon's fly ball to right didn't go all that far. In Fenway Park, nobody would have put down their beer to watch it travel, but at Yankee Stadium it had just enough energy to land softly in the first rows beyond the right-field fence, not fair by much, but fair by enough to make it 6–0.

After the grand slam, there were 7½ innings left to play, but the fight had gone out of the Yankees and the spirit had gone out of the sellout crowd. The game and ALCS were both spiritually over, if not officially, and the Red Sox had an upcoming date with the Cardinals.

7. October 4, 2003, Trot Nixon

Although their fans did not know it at the time, the fall of 2003 was the beginning of the end of the Red Sox's long decades without a world championship. Since Boston's ALCS title in 1986, it had played seven postseason series and lost six of them. Since they went ahead of the Mets 2–0 in the '86 World Series, the Red Sox had gone 6–26 in postseason play; the most recent two losses were to Oakland in the first two games of the 2003 Division Series.

Those games were in Oakland. The teams returned to Fenway Park on October 4 with the Athletics on the verge of sweeping Boston, as they had done in the 1988 ALCS and 1990 ALCS. Game 3 was a pitcher's duel, and went into extra innings at 1–1 mostly because Oakland lost two potential runs on bizarre plays in the sixth inning.

On one, Eric Byrnes was blocked off home plate by Jason Varitek as he tried to score, hurt his ankle, and did not get back to touch home plate before Varitek tagged him out. On the other, Miguel Tejada was tagged out as he casually trotted home after being awarded third base on obstruction by Bill Mueller; Tejada thought the call gave him home plate, too, but it did not and he was out.

Rich Harden came in to pitch for Oakland in the bottom of the eleventh. With one out, Doug Mirabelli singled to right. Grady Little sent up Trot Nixon to pinch-hit for Gabe Kapler and Nixon delivered Boston's first postseason pinch home run since Bernie Carbo in Game 6 of the '75 World Series.

The Red Sox won the game, 3–1. They won the next two games, including Game 5 in Oakland, to advance to the ALCS where they eventually lost another heartbreaking postseason series 4–3 this time to the Yankees.

However, starting with Game 3 of the 2003 Division Series, a game won by Nixon's homer, Boston won seven of its next nine postseason series and went 28–13 in its next 41 postseason games.

8. September 30, 1967, Carl Yastrzemski

The Red Sox came down to the final two games of the regular season in 1967 having to win both against the first-place Twins. It was, for Boston, the equivalent of two winner-take-all games, and it didn't matter which one it lost.

The next-to-last game was on a Saturday afternoon and it was a 2–2 game going into the bottom of the sixth. George Scott homered to center to make it 3–2 and it was still 3–2 when the Red Sox came to bat in the seventh. With one out, Mike Andrews reached on an infield hit, Jerry Adair on an error. That brought up Yastrzemski, and Minnesota manager Cal Ermer replaced Ron Kline with lefty reliever Jim Merritt to face Yaz.

Yastrzemski did it again. He drilled a three-run homer to right to give the Sox a 6–2 lead, the homer providing the winning runs as the Twins eventually came back to make it 6–4 on a Harmon Killebrew homer in the ninth.

9. September 4, 1988, Larry Parrish

The energy created by Morgan's Magic, when the Red Sox won 12 in a row and 19-of-20 after Joe Morgan replaced John McNamara as manager, finally ended and the 1988 season became trench warfare. Boston was in and out of first place in the AL East, battling with the Tigers, Yankees, and Brewers and in late August, the Sox embarked on a brutal road trip lasting 13 games.

The first 10 were on the West Coast, where they traditionally fared poorly, and after nine of those games Boston was 3–6. The last game of the West Coast segment was on Sunday, September 4, in Anaheim. Roger Clemens started for the Sox but wasn't especially effective. It was a 5–5 game after nine innings and the Angels had closer Bryan Harvey on the mound to start the tenth. Boston's leadoff batter that inning was Larry Parrish, the aging slugger that Lou Gorman had gotten as a free agent in July after he was released by the Rangers.

Parrish greeted Harvey with a shot to right-center that gave Boston an unexpected 6–5 lead. Lee Smith protected it with a scoreless bottom of the tenth and instead of leaving California with a 3–7 mark on the trip, the Sox were 4–6.

They went into that Sunday a game behind Detroit in the AL East race and as the Tigers lost that day, Boston had forged a tie for first. Parrish's homer got the Sox going on a hot stretch that saw them win 11-of-14. Once they tied Detroit for first that day in Anaheim, the Sox never lost the AL East lead.

"When I saw the ball disappear over the fence that day, I could feel this huge weight lifted from my shoulders," Boston right fielder Dwight Evans later said. Everyone else on the '88 Sox team seemed to feel the same way, and Boston eventually went on to one of its most memorable first-place finishes.

10. July 24, 2004, Bill Mueller

Bill Mueller is one of the most anonymous great players the Red Sox have ever had. Some of that was because of his pleasant, but bland nature. Some of it was because he played in the shadow of David Ortiz and Manny Ramirez. Some of it was because he was only great while he was in Boston.

But Mueller won a batting title with the Sox, became the first player to hit two grand slams in the same game from different sides of the plate, and belted a home run for the ages in a game for the ages in 2004.

The Yankees were at Fenway Park for a Saturday afternoon game having beaten Boston the night before, 8–7. In the third inning, Sox starter Bronson Arroyo hit Alex Rodriguez with a pitch, igniting a bench-clearing brawl that began when Jason Varitek pushed his glove into Rodriguez's face as he headed towards Arroyo.

Eventually, order was restored and New York went about the business of winning its second in a row over the Sox. The Yankees led 10–8 going into the bottom of the ninth and faced Mariano Rivera, naturally, who had come on to get the final out of the eighth inning.

A leadoff double by Nomar Garciaparra and a one-out single by Kevin Millar made it 10–9. Mueller came up with David McCarty, who had run for Millar on first. He also came up having hit 27 home runs in a Boston uniform, seven of them off Yankees pitching. He made it eight with a shot into the Red Sox bullpen, turning a 10–9 deficit into an 11–10 walk-off victory with one swing.

Legend has it that Mueller's thunderclap home run helped turn the Red Sox's season around, but it did not. Boston went 5–5 in the 10 games after Mueller's homer against Rivera and didn't really start to head up until after Garciaparra was traded at the end of the month.

Who knows, though, what effect the home run had on Rivera's thinking a little less than three months later, when he had to face Mueller in the ninth inning of Game 4 of the ALCS with the tying run on second base?

That is a subjective list of the Top Ten home runs in Red Sox history, but there are several others that were candidates for the list that didn't make it. They are in chronological order.

- August 20, 1967, Game 2—Jerry Adair's solo homer in the bottom of the eighth gives the Red Sox a 9–8 lead in a game they once trailed, 8–0.

- October 14, 1975—Dwight Evans' two-run homer off Rawly Eastwick in the top of the ninth of Game 3 of the World Series brings Boston into a 5–5 tie of a game it eventually lost in 10 innings, 6–5.

- October 25, 1986—Dave Henderson's solo home run off Rick Aguilera in the top of the tenth broke a 3–3 tie in Game 6 of the World Series. Boston later made it 5–3, but could not hold the lead.

- October 11, 1999—Troy O'Leary hits a three-run homer off Paul Shuey in the seventh inning at Jacobs Field to snap an 8–8 tie in a game the Red Sox won 12–8 to complete a comeback from two games down to beat Cleveland in the Division Series.

- May 28, 2000—Trot Nixon's two-run homer in the top of the ninth provides the only runs in the game as Pedro Martinez beats Roger Clemens 2–0 in an emotional early-season game at Yankee Stadium.

- September 1, 2003—Nixon's ninth-inning grand slam off Turk Wendell at Veterans Stadium in Philadelphia keyed a comeback 13–9 victory; the Sox trailed 9–7 going into the ninth. Boston won five in a row and 17-of-24 starting with that victory to nail down the American League Wild Card playoff spot.
- October 8, 2004—David Ortiz belts a two-run homer into the monster seats off Jarrod Washburn in the last of the tenth as Boston walks off with an 8–6 victory over the Angels and a sweep of the Division Series.
- October 19, 2004—Mark Bellhorn hits a three-run home run to left, originally called a double, to give the Red Sox a 4–0 lead in third inning of Game 6 of the 2004 ALCS in Yankee Stadium.
- October 23, 2004—Against Julian Tavarez, Bellhorn hits a two-run homer off Pesky's Pole at Fenway Park in the last of the eighth to snap a 9–9 tie and help Boston beat the Cardinals in Game 1 of the World Series.
- October 5, 2007—Manny Ramirez launches a mammoth three-run homer off Francisco Rodriguez and over the monster seats in the bottom of the ninth to give the Red Sox a 6–3 victory and 2–0 lead in the Division Series with the Angels.

ODDS & ENDS

On July 22, 1960, my father took me into Fenway Park so I could see Ted Williams play before he retired. Perhaps Williams would hit a home run that day. After all, he had hit 506 before that. And he did hit one, in the first inning, off Cleveland's Mudcat Grant to give the Sox a 1–0 lead. Even better, in the seventh Williams stole the last base of the 24 he had in his career. Boston won that game, 6–4.

* * *

On July 1, 1988, with the Red Sox at Royals Stadium in Kansas City, a place they had never played well in, catcher Rich Gedman came up with Todd Benzinger on first and stroked a long fly ball down the right-field line in the eighth inning. Was it fair or foul? The next sound was the "ping" of the ball striking the metal foul pole, followed by the sight of the ball detouring at an angle into the seats. First base umpire Dale Scott looked at the ball and the pole and signaled "foul ball"—no amount of arguing could change his mind. After the debates ended, Gedman grounded into a double play. What would have been a 9–8 Boston victory was an 8–7 loss.

* * *

On June 4, 1989, the Red Sox blew a 10-run lead in a game at Fenway Park. Behind shutout pitching by Mike Smithson, Boston had a 10–0 lead going into the top of the seventh. Smithson walked two batters to begin the inning, then had to leave with a pulled muscle. Bob Stanley relieved and Toronto got a couple of runs. They added four more in the eighth. In the ninth, Lee Smith gave up an RBI double to George Bell and a grand slam to Ernie Whitt as the Jays took an 11–10 lead.

Boston got a run in the last of the ninth and had the winning run on second when Marty Barrett grounded out; in doing so, Barrett tripped near the bag at first base and suffered what amounted to a career-ending knee injury. Toronto won the game 13–11 as Junior Felix hit a two-run homer off Dennis Lamp in the thirteenth inning.

* * *

On August 22, 1989, the Sox were playing a rather unimportant series at Yankee Stadium and utility man Randy Kutcher entered the game in the seventh to give Wade Boggs a rest at third. In the top of the eighth, Kutcher hit an opposite-field home run into the bleachers in right-center to give Boston a 4–3 lead. A fan threw the ball back onto the field and it landed near right fielder Jesse Barfield, who possessed a legendary arm. Disgusted, Barfield picked the ball up and threw it over the bleachers, over the facade atop the back wall of the ballpark, and out onto River Avenue. Imagine someone walking along the street, seeing a baseball land on the concrete, and thinking he had just seen the longest home run in baseball history.

In the bottom of the inning, with Rob Murphy pitching for the Sox, a fan walked down to the bottom row of the third deck, stepped over the railing, and jumped onto the screen behind home plate. The screen held and the fan began jumping around on it before security and the police coaxed him off and put him in cuffs.

Murphy described his reaction to seeing the fan climb the railing, "I said to myself—'Hmmm, this could be interesting.'" Murphy wound up as the winning pitcher.

* * *

On April 25, 1990, Bill Buckner hit the only inside-the-park home run of his career after hitting 173 regulation ones. In the fourth inning of a game against the Angels at Fenway Park, Buckner—back with the

Sox for a second tour of duty—hit a fly ball into the right-field corner. Angels outfielder Claudell Washington went back to fence and, in an attempt to make the catch, tumbled over it and into the first row of box seats. Washington got stuck there. As the ball lay on the warning track, Buckner, 40 years old and with aching ankles, circled the bases for his only inside-the-park homer, and the last home run of his career.

* * *

On September 1, 1990, Mike Greenwell hit a ground ball over the first-base bag at Fenway Park that turned into a grand-slam home run. With the bases loaded and nobody out in the fifth, Boston lead the Yankees 5–1 and Greenwell faced New York southpaw Greg Cadaret, who was looking for a ground ball and got one, except it went right down the foul line.

Normally, it would have been a double, but as Yankees right fielder Jesse Barfield ran over to cut it off near the foul pole, he stopped dead in his tracks. Barfield had pulled a hamstring and couldn't move. The ball went past him and rolled all the way along the curve of the right-field fence and Greenwell crossed home plate standing up.

* * *

On April 22, 1994, Sox right fielder Billy Hatcher stole home. Red Sox players have occasionally been credited with steals of home plate on the back end of a double steal, but not since Hatcher has a Boston player stolen home simply by outrunning the pitch.

It happened with two out in the bottom of the seventh with the Sox trailing the Angels 5–4 and lefty Chuck Finley on the mound. Hatcher took off on a 3–1 pitch and was safe by plenty to tie the score. Boston eventually won, 6–5. Asked after the game if he knew Hatcher was going on the play, Sox manager Butch Hobson said he was not sure until he saw Hatcher take his lead.

"I think he's fixin' to steal home," was Hobson's observation, and he was right.

* * *

On June 14, 1992, at the SkyDome in Toronto, Boston reliever Danny Darwin allowed four inherited runners to score in the sixth inning of a game the Blue Jays won, 6–2. Darwin took over for Boston starter Mike Gardiner with one out, the bases loaded, and a 2–0 count on Kelly Gruber. Darwin threw two more balls and Gruber walked forcing in a run, but by rule the walk was charged to Gardiner. John Olerud followed with a three-run double to clear the bases and added three more inherited runs to Darwin's total for the inning.

* * *

On August 1, 2002, at The Ballpark in Texas, Red Sox pitcher Frank Castillo surrendered home runs for the cycle. The Rangers had knocked Boston starter John Burkett out of the game with one out in the second inning and Castillo came in to try to give manager Grady Little some blowout innings. In that second inning, Castillo served up a grand slam to former Sox miscreant Carl Everett to make it 12–1; in the third, Kevin Mench hit a solo home run to make it 13–1; then Todd Hollandsworth hit a three-run homer and it was 16–1. Mike Lamb finished the cycle in the fifth with a two-run homer to make it 18–1. The Rangers wound up winning, 19–7.

* * *

On July 29, 2003, at Texas, Bill Mueller not only hit a home run from both sides of the plate—he hit a grand slam from both sides, becoming the first player in history to do so. Mueller hit his first in the seventh inning off lefty Aaron Fultz, then another in the eighth off righty Jay Powell. Mueller had also hit a solo home run off R.A. Dickey in the third and finished the night with nine RBIs in a 14–7 Red Sox victory.

* * *

On September 14, 2005, in Toronto, the Red Sox trailed the Blue Jays 2–1 going into the fifth inning. With two out, Gabe Kapler reached on an error by Toronto third baseman Corey Koskie. Tony Graffanino followed with a home run to left field. Kapler, not sure if Graffanino's ball was a home run, ran hard from first, but as he rounded second, went down in an agonized heap. Kapler had ruptured his left Achilles tendon.

Graffanino had the presence of mind to not pass Kapler, who was eventually taken from the game on a utility cart. Sent in to pinch-run for him was—and this name is the answer to one of the all-time great trivia questions in Red Sox history—Alejandro Machado, which was perfectly legal according to the rules of baseball. In this case, the rule said, "If an accident to a runner is such as to prevent him from proceeding to a base to which he is entitled, as on a home run hit out of the playing field, or an award of one or more bases, a substitute runner shall be permitted to complete the play."

It took about five minutes before Kapler got back up, helped to his feet by Sox trainers, and he asked if he could limp around the bases with some help and finish the play. "It's embarrassing to be out there and not be able to finish it," Kapler said. "So, I would've liked to be able to at least run around the bases. But they told me that wasn't the right thing to do."

Machado got credit for the run scored, his first in the majors, and the Red Sox went on to win the game, 5–3. Kapler missed the rest of the 2005 season but returned to action midway through the 2006 campaign.

REFERENCES

I covered my first Red Sox game for the *Worcester Telegram* in 1987 and have kept a scrapbook of all Sox box scores, with occasional notations, since then. That proved to be a major source of material for this book.

Beyond that, there remains no better source for baseball history in general than the online site "Retrosheet"—the information provided there was crucial. As a member of the Society of Baseball Research, I also used its online encyclopedia, particularly in tracking down Clyde Vollmer's home runs.

No Red Sox fan, nor anyone who covers the team, should be without *The Curse of the Bambino* by Dan Shaughnessy or *Red Sox Century* by Glenn Stout and Dick Johnson. Both books are invaluable in understanding the history of the franchise and were invaluable in putting together this particular book.

The Red Sox were generous in letting me peruse their collection of box scores and clippings and I researched some of the team's long-ago past via microfilm editions of my paper, the *Worcester Telegram & Gazette*.